The
GREAT GOLF COURSES OF CANADA

The
GREAT GOLF COURSES OF CANADA

by John Gordon
Photography by Michael French

McGraw-Hill Ryerson

Toronto   Montreal

Spalding Canada

Toronto

First published in 1991 by
McGraw-Hill Ryerson Limited

Front cover photograph of the Victoria Golf Club by Alan Jennick. Courtesy of the British Columbia Ministry of Tourism.

ISBN 0-07-551105-3

Design and compilation © 1991
Canadian Golf Press Inc.
250 The Esplanade, Suite 205
Toronto, Ontario M5A 1J2

Distribution to bookstores and libraries
McGraw-Hill Ryerson
300 Water Street
Whitby, Ontario L1N 9B6

Distribution to the golf trade
Spalding Canada
250 Courtland Avenue
Concord, Ontario L4K 4N3

Corporate Marketing
The Sports Marketing Group
Toronto, Ontario.

Canadian Cataloguing in Publication Data

Gordon, John (John William)
  The great golf courses of Canada

ISBN 0-07-551105-3

1. Golf courses - Canada. I. Title.

GV975.G67 1991   796.352′06871   C90-094182-0

Printed and bound in Canada by D.W. Friesen Printing

To my wife, Leslie,
and my children, Will and Alexandra.
They, along with my mother and father,
were there every step of the way,
if not in body, at least in spirit.

ACKNOWLEDGEMENTS

Heartfelt thanks go to some friends and colleagues: Bill Ironstone, who introduced me to the game; Lorne Rubenstein, who got me into this author business; James Fitchette, who bailed me out on a couple of obvious occasions; Bob Weeks, for sharing his expertise on the Weston Club; Glencoe expert John Down, and Royal Ottawa historian Robert Majoribanks.

I have endeavored to credit all sources within the text and apologize for unintentional oversights. In addition to the individuals named above, many non-bylined articles in back issues of SCORE, Canada's golf magazine, from 1981 to 1990, were used as reference material. The published and unpublished club histories of the following clubs, used with their permission, also provided valuable material: Beaconsfield, Brantford, Calgary, Capilano, Essex, Highlands Links, London Hunt, Mississauga, Royal Colwood, Scarboro, Shaughnessy, St. Charles, Summit, Toronto and Westmount. Ralph Costello's book, "The First Fifty Years", was also of assistance.

Almost without exception, the head professionals, general managers and other staff of the clubs mentioned in this book, and others that aren't, were gracious and generous with their knowledge and hospitality.

Thank you to Spalding Canada for their support in getting this book distributed out to the golf trade market, hopefully where all Canadian golf enthusiasts will get an opportunity to see it.

Without the invaluable support of the Canadian Professional Golfers' Association, representing 2000 members from coast to coast, this book would not have been possible. My thanks to David Colling and his very capable and helpful staff.

My employers at SCORE deserve special mention because without their forbearance I would not have been able to write this.

Above all, a salute to my wife Leslie (Ironstone) Gordon for editing the manuscript and providing invaluable advice and support throughout the writing process; and to my publisher, Jim Williamson, without whom this book would never have been done.

TABLE OF CONTENTS

INTRODUCTION

Why 38 golf courses? Why not 138? Or 1,038 for that matter? No doubt this book could have been titled "Just a Few of the Great Golf Courses of Canada." In travelling from Vancouver Island to Newfoundland to research this book, two things have become undeniable: that Canada is blessed with exceptional golf courses from coast to coast, and that identifying your favorite layout is as subjective as choosing your spouse. Golf, the game played by millions around the world for hundreds of years, remains the most personal of pursuits.

The Great Golf Courses of Canada was intended as a sampler, not a ranking, of the fantastic array of courses in this country. Of the more than 2,000 layouts we have to choose from, the ones in this book represent only a smidgen of the cream.

Of course, you will find the obvious, although it is almost certainly presumptuous to say they would be on everyone's list: Glen Abbey, home of the Canadian Open and perhaps the most renowned course in the country; The National Golf Club, arguably the toughest layout; history-laden courses such as Victoria Golf Club, Calgary, Toronto, Royal Montreal and New Brunswick's Riverside.

But one of the many joys of researching and writing *The Great Golf Courses of Canada* was discovering for myself the wonders of hidden jewels ranging from Wolf Creek in

Alberta to Nova Scotia's New Ashburn and Highlands Links. No doubt you have others that, in your estimation, deserve special mention.

These selections were not made without careful thought and consideration of input from a cross-country panel which contributes to the biannual selection of the top 25 golf courses in Canada for SCORE, Canada's Golf Magazine. The initial list was provided by the Canadian Professional Golfers' Association and was refined with the help of golfers from coast to coast.

Almost without exception, I played or, at the very least, toured every golf course featured in this book. As a result, I can testify that the stunning photographs by Michael French are the next best thing to actually visiting and playing these courses. The ultimate goal of *The Great Golf Courses of Canada* is to offer every reader a richly satisfying and stimulating experience through the combination of Michael's pictures and my words.

Whether you are a member of one of the clubs included in this book, an avid golfer interested in seeing what pleasures stretch from coast to coast, or a novice who is trying to understand what this golf fuss is all about, you will enjoy The Great Golf Courses of Canada. Maybe not as much as I enjoyed writing it, but it will be close.

Every hole at Banff features the natural beauty of the Rockies.

BANFF SPRINGS

Golf Course

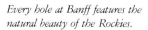

Architects: Stanley Thompson (18)
Bill Robinson (9)
Head Professional: Doug Wood
Manager: Stan Bishop
Superintendent: Bernie Thiesen

Banff Springs, it is said, was the first golf course to cost $1 million to build. The original 18 holes represented a test of man using machinery to mould nature to his purposes rather than fighting it into submission. "Nature must always be the architect's model," said course designer Stanley Thompson. Despite those sentiments, there was no avoiding the fact the thousands of tons of rock had to be blasted and hundreds of trees had to be sacrificed to create this masterpiece which came into being in 1927. So skilful was this act of creation that, in maturity, the course appears one with nature.

Those 18 holes now are labelled the Rundle and Sulphur nines, while another nine, Tunnel, was designed by Bill Robinson of British Columbia and put into play in 1989. "We tried to make it as similar to the old course as we could," Robinson said. The three nines are played in various combinations, but it is the original 18 of which golfers speak with reverence. The setting is unparalleled. In the shadow of Mount Rundle, Sulphur Mountain and Tunnel Mountain, the holes stretch along the Bow River within the confines of Banff National Park. The beauty of the course and the surrounding terrain are breathtaking: pine forests, crystal-clear water, snowy

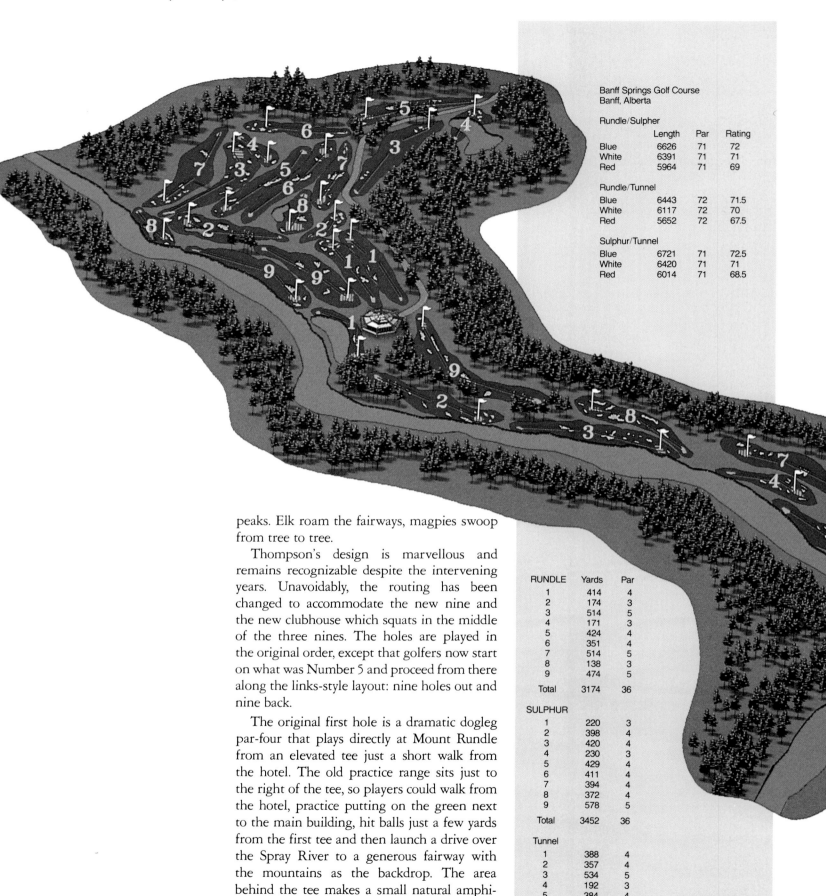

Banff Springs Golf Course
Banff, Alberta

Rundle/Sulpher

	Length	Par	Rating
Blue	6626	71	72
White	6391	71	71
Red	5964	71	69

Rundle/Tunnel

Blue	6443	72	71.5
White	6117	72	70
Red	5652	72	67.5

Sulphur/Tunnel

Blue	6721	71	72.5
White	6420	71	71
Red	6014	71	68.5

peaks. Elk roam the fairways, magpies swoop from tree to tree.

Thompson's design is marvellous and remains recognizable despite the intervening years. Unavoidably, the routing has been changed to accommodate the new nine and the new clubhouse which squats in the middle of the three nines. The holes are played in the original order, except that golfers now start on what was Number 5 and proceed from there along the links-style layout: nine holes out and nine back.

The original first hole is a dramatic dogleg par-four that plays directly at Mount Rundle from an elevated tee just a short walk from the hotel. The old practice range sits just to the right of the tee, so players could walk from the hotel, practice putting on the green next to the main building, hit balls just a few yards from the first tee and then launch a drive over the Spray River to a generous fairway with the mountains as the backdrop. The area behind the tee makes a small natural amphitheatre where other golfers or guests could watch the proceedings. This fine starting hole now is the 15th.

The former finishing hole (now the 14th,

RUNDLE	Yards	Par
1	414	4
2	174	3
3	514	5
4	171	3
5	424	4
6	351	4
7	514	5
8	138	3
9	474	5
Total	3174	36

SULPHUR		
1	220	3
2	398	4
3	420	4
4	230	3
5	429	4
6	411	4
7	394	4
8	372	4
9	578	5
Total	3452	36

Tunnel		
1	388	4
2	357	4
3	534	5
4	192	3
5	384	4
6	474	5
7	382	4
8	134	3
9	424	4
Total	3268	36

or the fifth of the Sulphur nine) is a strong dogleg par-four measuring 429 yards from the blues with more than two dozen bunkers all told. Some of these bunkers protect the driving area, some threaten faulty approaches, where others guard three sides of the green. The hole plays into the prevailing wind, so the second shot must often be a fairway wood or long-iron. The magnificent presence of the Banff Springs Hotel looms in the distance: a perfect home hole. With the new arrangement, the finishing hole is the old Number 4, a par-five, and no slouch at 580 yards from the blues with plenty of bunkers, mounds and swales.

The fairways at Banff Springs feature many sweeping contours to make drives and second shots challenging. Many fairways are bordered by mounds that tend to bring off-line drives back into play. Driving areas are moderately wide in most places, but the smart golfer will try to play to a particular location in the fairway to set up a favorable angle to the green. The contouring of the fairways and greens echoes the meandering movement of the Bow River and the surrounding terrain at the base of the mountains.

Most greens are canted toward the approaching golfer to receive incoming shots and many are raised above the level of the fairway. The golfer usually has the option of rolling the ball onto the greens; often the sole approach method for high-handicappers. The greens are not large by modern standards, although their size varies appropriately according to the shot the golfer is expected to play. They have many subtle contours and breaks that make three-footers treacherous, but they are not gimmicky.

The most memorable feature of Banff Springs is the bunkering. Most of the bunkers are located in or on mounds, and they feature flashed faces to make them visible from afar. As one approaches them, they change their shape and appearance, revealing new facets from different angles, just as the appearance of the surrounding mountains changes when seen from different angles or in different light.

Mis-hit approach shots tend to migrate into greenside bunkers, and certain key fairways bunkers also seem to attract off-line balls. Many fairway bunkers serve to catch errant shots and save them from the woods, while others indicate the preferred line: drive over them safely

The "Little Bow" — another of Thompson's inspired par-threes.

The famed "Cauldron" at Banff Springs plays 171 yards over a mountain lake.

and you have a good angle for approaching the green. The bunkers are contoured such that the ball tends to roll down the face; one is never confronted with an "impossible" bunker shot.

The most exciting single shot is probably the tee shot at Number 4, the "Devil's Cauldron". The tee is quite elevated compared to the sloping green that is carved into the hillside about 170 yards away. The shot must carry over a glacial lake to the green, a shelf about 15 feet above the water level. Mount Rundle watches on the right. Club selection is tricky here: on a calm day, a smooth eight-iron; in the wind, use your imagination.

Banff's high elevation, more than 1,600 metres above sea level, means that the ball flies farther, perhaps one-to-two clubs' differ-

ence. On the other hand, the wind varies from imperceptible to gale-force, meaning that downwind par-fours in excess of 400 yards can be played driver-wedge. As well, the mountain backdrops tend to distort one's perspective, making the business of judging distances a memorable experience, to say the least. The story is told of Gene Sarazen who ignored the advice of his local caddie, chose a club on his own, and barely made it halfway to the green.

The century-old Banff Springs Hotel, with more than 800 rooms, is a massive edifice that looks like a noble's castle in the Alps. The lobby and parts of the mezzanine are dark with heavy furniture; in places, it looks like a medieval fortress. The "new" addition was built in the 1920s and has recently received multi-million-dollar renovations.

Stanley Thompson was a genius at designing par-threes. Here, the 138-yard "Papoose."

Stanley Thompson (1894-1952)

Stanley Thompson was one of five brothers, all of whom achieved notoriety in golfing circles. Brothers Frank and Bill won the Canadian Amateur, Nicol was the head professional at Hamilton Golf and Country Club and Matt was a pro in Western Canada. Stanley, while a formidable player (he claimed the medalist title in the 1923 Canadian Amateur qualifying with a set of borrowed clubs), would become recognized as the dean of Canadian golf course architects. His memorials range literally from one coast of Canada to the other, from Capilano in West Vancouver to Highlands Links on Cape Breton Island. In between, he created masterpieces such as Jasper Park, Westmount, St. George's and a multitude of others. Banff, one of his crowning achievements, has the dubious distinction of being the first course in the world to cost more than $1 million to build. Thompson was one of three founders of the American Society of Golf Course Architects. The others were Donald Ross and Robert Trent Jones, at one time Thompson's junior partner.

*Calgary has changed very little
from the 1920s design and can
easily be played in four hours.*

Calgary, Alberta

CALGARY

Golf and Country Club

*Architect: Willie Park Jr.
Head Professional: Al Ewen
Manager: Jim Sherlock
Superintendent: Lockie Shaw*

The nomadic development of the Calgary Golf and Country Club parallels in many ways the growth patterns of the city of Calgary and the Canadian West. A small band of sports-minded individuals scattered nine crude golf holes across the prairie near the lifeline of the area, the Canadian Pacific Railway tracks, back in 1897. For the next dozen years, these golfing pioneers, who held no title on the land and were viewed as sporting squatters, were forced to pick up their hickory-shafted clubs and gutta percha balls and move as Calgary expanded.

Although the city of Calgary is just more than 100 years old, its people have established a reputation for resourcefulness and persistence that has stood the Calgary Golf and Country Club in good stead. In 1897, the town was home to about 4,000 souls, some of whom may not have been as enthusiastic about founding a golf club had they known the tribulations that awaited.

By 1899, just two years after establishing the original course, the growing community was beginning to intrude and the decision was made to relocate. Apparently, the existing clubhouse was simply hauled to a new site farther south, and nine more holes were dug. Three years later, another forced retreat again put wheels under

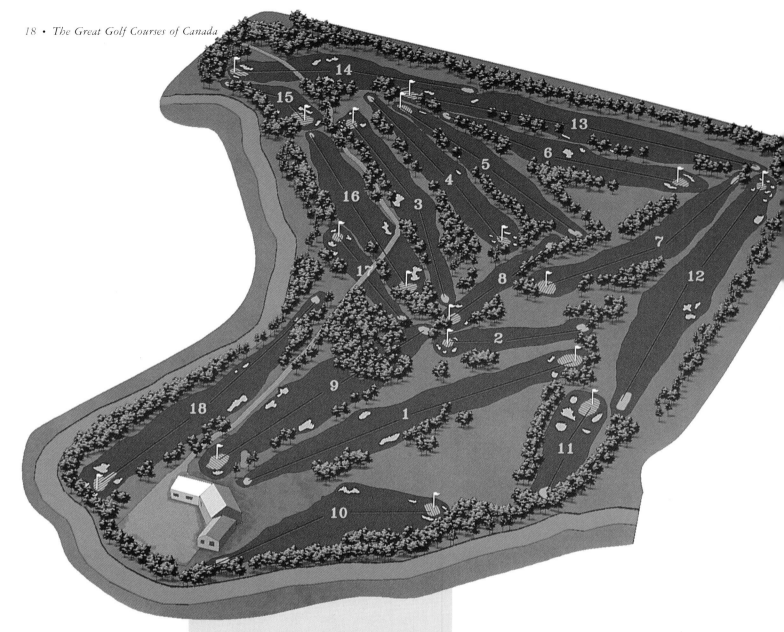

Calgary Golf and Country Club
Calgary, Alberta

	Length	Par	Rating
Blue	6449	70	71
White	6191	70/73	70/73
Red	5492	70/71	66.5/70

Hole	Yards	Par
1	463	5
2	184	3
3	439	4
4	401	4
5	407	4
6	390	4
7	411	4
8	220	3
9	353	4
OUT	3258	35
10	291	4
11	168	3
12	585	5
13	574	5
14	375	4
15	168	3
16	400	4
17	199	3
18	456	4
IN	3191	35
Total	6449	70

the clubhouse. This time, the level of sophistication had ascended to barbed wire around the square sand greens to dissuade grazing cattle from roaming across them.

Incorporated in 1906 by the provincial legislature — itself just one year old — as the Calgary Golf Club, the membership decided that these itinerant ways were no longer appropriate and set out to purchase a permanent residence for the club. Once the land was acquired, the Calgary Golf and Country Club came into being to "promote the physical welfare of the members and encourage the game of golf, tennis, bowling and other games, hunting, or any form of exercise, and for social purposes." A new course was laid out and construction of a new clubhouse begun.

In 1911, one year before the first Calgary Stampede, the new golf club was officially opened. It had a primitive watering system

for its grass greens, but to get to the putting surfaces, members had to trek across hardpan prairie pocked with gopher holes. To the credit of the determined membership, this situation did not last long.

Famed Scottish architect Willie Park Jr. was contacted in 1921 and agreed to redesign the course, a task that was completed between 1923 and 1925. By the time his renovations were complete, the layout was one of the finest in the country. This achievement was crowned by the fact that the Calgary Golf and Country Club had become the first course in Canada that watered fairways. These fairways were, however, virgin prairie and it was not until 1935 that a concerted effort was made to improve the soil through the addition of loam and manure — an effective, though odiferous, method. Grass tees with automatic sprinklers were also installed at this time.

Such improvements have continued on a layout that has changed very little from Park's original design. Short by modern standards at 6,400 yards from the back tees, this consummate members' course is a shotmaker's delight, with many holes bounded by mature trees. The course is extremely well groomed, meaning that an errant shot can usually be located easily and advanced toward the hole. And, since it's built on only 126 acres, the walks between green and tee are brief.

"A round here seldom takes more than four hours," says Al Ewen, head professional here for 26 years, "even though we are an extremely busy club, doing about 40,000 rounds a year." Ewen cites the third, fourth and fifth holes as key to a good round at Calgary Golf and Country Club. "All three are very difficult par-fours that put the emphasis on the tee shot. If you don't hit a good drive, you'll be hitting

Compact and well-groomed, Calgary's priority is to provide enjoyment for its members.

Calgary's par-threes are generally long and hazardous.

long-irons or fairway woods into small greens all day."

The third is the Number 1 handicap hole, a 340-yard par-four, where your tee shot must carry a valley some 200 yards out. Otherwise, it's at least a long-iron into a tough-to-hit green. The same valley comes into play on the fourth, says Ewen. "You have to hit it into the flat, otherwise you've got a downhill lie onto an elevated green — a difficult shot. The fifth hole is less than 400 yards, but you've got to get the ball off the tee. The second shot is a mid-to long-iron through a very narrow entrance between lines of fir trees."

Just as vital to scoring well here are the last three holes. The 16th is a straightaway 381-yard par-four with a very narrow landing area. "This hole plays one more club, at least," advises Ewen. "It runs slightly uphill, even though it doesn't appear to." The par-three 17th stretches 193 yards from the members' tees across a precipitous ravine and a roadway. And the highly elevated tee of the fine finishing hole at Calgary provides a panoramic view of the area. Don't be too intimidated by the tee shot, consoles Ewen. "Even though it appears to be a very long carry to hit the fairway, it's only about 170 yards from the white tees."

A Look Back

Notes from the Calgary Golf and Country Club's comprehensive and well-written club history, prepared on the occasion of the club's 75th anniversary in 1972:

1914 — "Members are forbidden to purchase balls from caddies. Is it possible that caddies became sharper of eye and fewer balls were lost when the incentives of free enterprise were squelched?"

1914 — "Club's financial statement included an item of $13.40 for goat medals." Goat medals?

1915 — "It was resolved that the club purchase from the Hudson's Bay Co. 36 gallons of Kilmarnock Scotch Whiskey at a price of $4.50 a gallon."

1920 — The board of management decides to move the pro shop from the garage to the stable and will pay for the materials necessary for the alternations, but the pro must do the work.

1920 — "Sheets of the guest register bearing the signatures of the Prince of Wales and party have been removed by some person unknown."

1945 — "E.S. Doughty reported that his certificate for one share of stock had been seized by the Japanese and asked that the fact be noted."

1957 — "Resolved: that ladies' slacks be prohibited from use on the course and in the clubhouse at all times . . ."

1969 — "Rule 20 regulating ladies' dress was deleted. The informality of the times was evident."

The 574-yard 13th hole is the longest on the course and is the toughest hole on the back nine.

The par-three seventh hole on the Glen Forest course reveals some of the course's trademarks: a multitude of bunkers.

GLENCOE

Golf and Country Club

Architect: Robert Trent Jones Jr.
Head Professional: Don Price
Manager: Jim Powell
Superintendent: Ken Olsvik

In the beginning, there were dirt, weeds and trees. But there was a specific character to the foliage, indicating someone had taken great care and time to map out the valley for 36 great golf holes. They were the remnants of grandiose dreams: the finest fairways in the land, for the exclusive use of the upper crust. Something went amiss, and the project died. The stillborn Spruce Vale Golf Club went into receivership in 1981.

"Someone mentioned the course was available . . . it was the late spring of '83," recalls Glencoe Golf and Country Club manager Jim Powell. "We weren't really even looking at a golf course. But after we went out and had a look at it in the fall, we went back to the board and started putting some numbers together." In that rather offhand manner, the Glencoe Club, an existing multi-sport facility, officially rescued one of Robert Trent Jones

Jr.'s finer pieces of work from receivership in 1984 for $4.8 million.

"Under the new owners' influence, the golf course really took off," says superintendent Ken Olsvik, who had been on the property since May 1983 with a five-man crew. "We had 16 fairways and 12 greens. We recovered the irrigation system and were maintaining what was there for the Royal Bank." The bank was the major receiver and, although there were a number of bids to take over the property, no one could match the resources and strength of the Glencoe bid.

"We went to our members in February of '84 and the voted an overwhelming majority to go for it," says Powell, who has been with the club since 1963. "The only stipulation was that we sign up 400 golf members inside the deadline and we made it easily." The bulk of the financing was raised through $5,000 entry

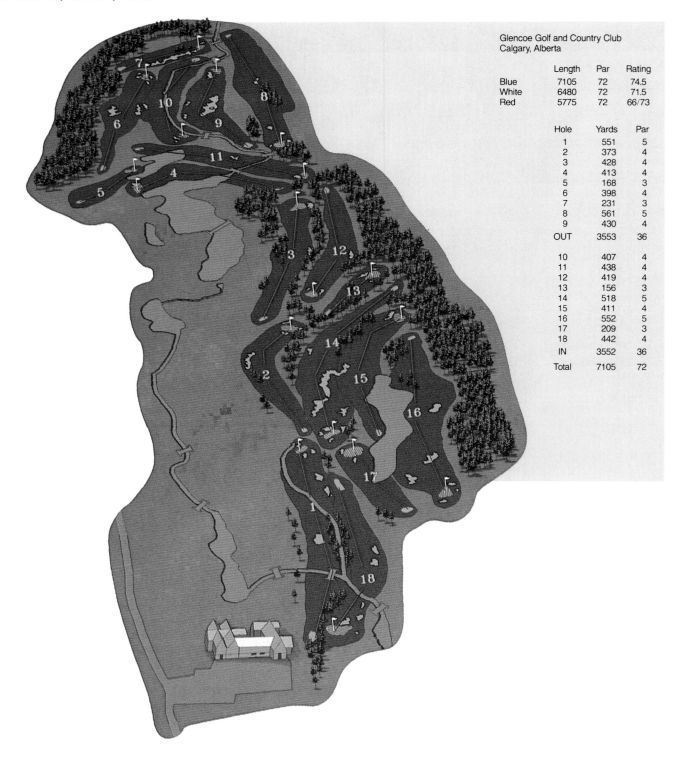

Glencoe Golf and Country Club
Calgary, Alberta

	Length	Par	Rating
Blue	7105	72	74.5
White	6480	72	71.5
Red	5775	72	66/73

Hole	Yards	Par
1	551	5
2	373	4
3	428	4
4	413	4
5	168	3
6	398	4
7	231	3
8	561	5
9	430	4
OUT	3553	36
10	407	4
11	438	4
12	419	4
13	156	3
14	518	5
15	411	4
16	552	5
17	209	3
18	442	4
IN	3552	36
Total	7105	72

fees. In 1990, it would have cost twice that, just to get on the 150-person waiting list. There are 900 active members playing the 36 holes, which is a testament to long hours of hard work by Olsvik and his 30-man staff, and to a club full of gung-ho members. "You can't credit any one person," argues Powell, who works for a young membership whose average age is 42. "I think what made it work was the club."

All 18 holes of the 7,105-yard Glen Forest course, rated 2.5 strokes tougher than its par 72, opened for play in the fall of 1984. The 6,500-yard, par-70 Glen Meadows course opened nine holes in July 1985 and the final nine that fall. The clubhouse went up the following April. "It was just a case of finishing off everything," says Powell, who estimates the club has invested close to $12 million in the layout. "We're still finishing, polishing here and there. But looking back, we're very pleased with the way everything has gone. We've never had to assess our members."

Olsvik says it was just a case of putting in the time, once the club was on a sound financial footing. "We never changed any design features. We just had to plant the grass, create the bunkers and rebuild the water system." And while all that was getting underway, the club raided nearby Canyon Meadows for Head Professional Don Price to reorganize the pro shop and golfing programs.

"The quality of the course sold me right from the first time I played it," Price asserts. He now has four assistants manning the pro shop, along with part-time clerical staff. "I decided I wanted to be a part of it as it developed and grew."

Price had to deal with a number of unique situations immediately; such as adjusting to the flow of traffic for a 36-hole course, hiring the proper number of staff to deal with double the normal membership and teaching raw rookies how to play the game at a reasonable level in order to maintain an acceptable pace of play on a difficult championship golf course. For although there are two 18-hole layouts at Glencoe, most golfers headed straight for the merciless Glen Forest 18. This course is, as indicated by its name, heavily treed and features a multitude of bunkers and lots of water.

"Another initial problem with the Forest opening a year earlier was that a lot of golfers didn't want to get pushed over to the Meadows," says Price. "A lot of people thought the Meadows was going to be the ladies' course, so we initially had trouble getting even play. But the Meadows came along quickly and pretty soon everyone discovered it was certainly worth playing, too."

The best of the Meadows, a shorter, much more open track, is yet to come, say the folks

The fifth tee of the Glen Forest course offers a glimpse of several other holes.

Of Glencoe's 36 holes, the Glen Forest course is the more heavily wooded although, as shown here, the Glen Meadows 18 has its share of trees as well.

Hole #1: 551 yards par 5

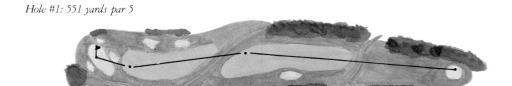

The Toughest Hole at Glencoe

The player who decides to challenge the endurance test known as the Glen Forest course will have little time to warm up because the first hole is also the Number 1-rated stroke hole. A par-five that plays 551 yards from the blue tees and 510 from the whites, this treacherous hole is lined with trees and pitted with enormous bunkers. It demands a precise tee shot between the large bunker on the left and the water and trees to the right. The second shot should be a layout left of the two-tiered, well-bunkered green.

at Glencoe. Olsvik and company are carrying out an aggressive tree-planting program there because "we think of it as an alpine course rather than a links course," says the super-intendent. "We're not trying to take the country out of the property. We're just trying to blend it in with the natural resources. The strength of Glencoe is going to take this course a long way. We're not going to make any changes just for the sake of making changes, but we can certainly improve it."

Price figures golfers have yet to see the best of all 36 holes in what he refers to as "Paradise Valley." "It's changed so much in the past two or three years, it's scary," he says. "It's going to get better and better as the years progress.

I've always felt it takes 10 years to get into maturity so we're only about halfway there."

Glencoe is not doing too badly for being only halfway there. The Glen Forest course drew rave reviews from Canadian Tour players who tested it in the 1989 Canadian PGA Championship, eventually won by Jean-Louis Lamarre of Quebec with a 13-under-par 275 total. It was the first major championship at the course which has since played host to the 1990 Alberta Amateur. "I was amazed at the way the pros played the course," analyzed Price. "They hit a lot of irons off the tee, not really concerned with the distance, even though it plays 7,100 yards from the tips. They played it in a very patient manner."

The predominance of trees provides attractive setting for greens such as the Glen Meadows' 14th.

The dogleg 14th at Jasper Park challenges the player to cut off as much of the lake as he dares.

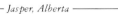

— Jasper, Alberta —

JASPER PARK LODGE

Golf Course

Architect: Stanley Thompson
Head Professional: Ron MacLeod
Manager: Perry Cooper
Superintendent: Brian Hill

Jasper Park's classic 18-hole course was designed by Canada's greatest architect, Stanley Thompson, and opened for play in 1925. This splendid resort is located in Jasper National Park in the heart of the Rockies, just outside the town of Jasper on Lac Beauvert, where the water is green and clear. Nearby looms a range of rugged peaks called the Whistlers. The course winds through pine woods, affording golfers stunning views of the surrounding snow-capped mountains, which form a backdrop for most of the holes. Jasper Park's main challenges are the wind, the undulating fairways, the tricky greens and the fascinating bunkers.

The course sits close to the main lodge and some of the cabins. The practice range is 10 metres from the first tee and it is long enough for Greg Norman's longest drives. The holes move in an essentially circular pattern clockwise. Thus, the golfer's orientation with respect to the wind changes subtly from hole to hole; it is never really the same from one to the next. The course is a pleasant walk, with tees close by previous greens in all instances, and the elevation above sea level (about 1,000 metres) is not so extreme that one becomes winded because of the thin mountain air.

The holes are gently contoured with soft sweeping lines that

are most inviting and interesting to behold. Trees line both sides of many fairways, but landing areas are, for the most part, generous. Still, there are clearly preferred sides of the fairways if one hopes to have an advantageous line into the greens, which themselves tend to be medium-sized to smallish and set at angles to the fairways. They tend to be canted toward the approaching golfer and many are slightly elevated.

The front entrance to every green is open to allow running approach shots. Some greens, however, are raised enough that most successful approaches will fly all the way to the putting surface. The 16th green is guarded in front by water for more than three-quarters of its width; but a running shot to the extreme right side of the fairway could find the putting surface, if played to perfection.

The most notable feature of the course, after the spectacular setting, is Thompson's incomparable bunkering. His use of sand, here and at Banff Springs four hours to the south, could serve as a doctoral course in the fine art of

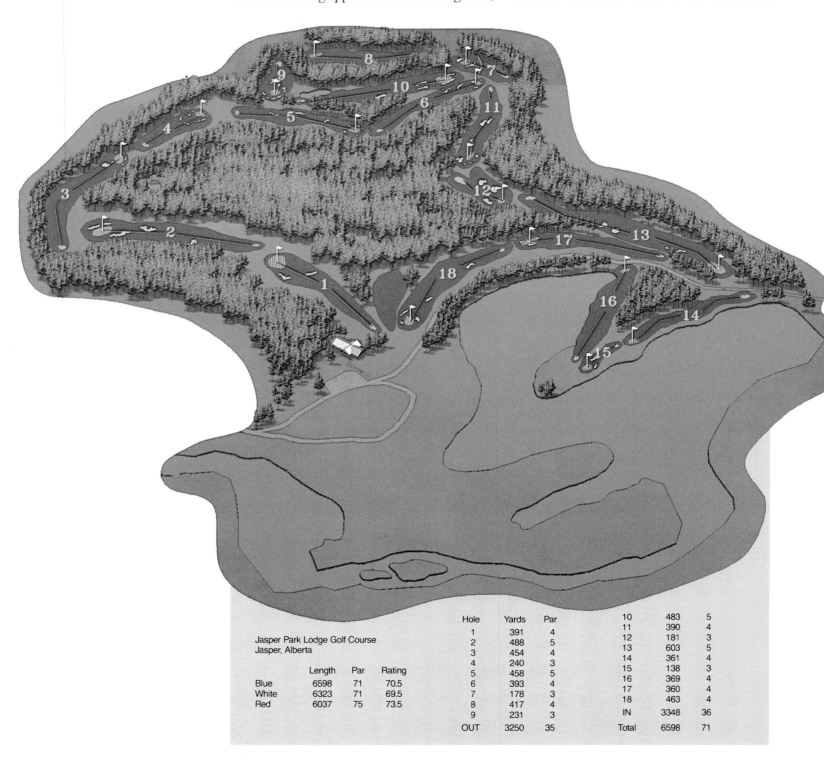

Hole	Yards	Par
1	391	4
2	488	5
3	454	4
4	240	3
5	458	5
6	393	4
7	178	3
8	417	4
9	231	3
OUT	3250	35

Hole	Yards	Par
10	483	5
11	390	4
12	181	3
13	603	5
14	361	4
15	138	3
16	369	4
17	360	4
18	463	4
IN	3348	36
Total	6598	71

Jasper Park Lodge Golf Course
Jasper, Alberta

	Length	Par	Rating
Blue	6598	71	70.5
White	6323	71	69.5
Red	6037	75	73.5

bunkering to frame fairways and greens, to provide interesting tactical and strategic challenges, and to enhance the beauty of an already gorgeous setting. The bunkers at Jasper Park are beautifully shaped and their appearance changes depending on the angle from which they are viewed. As you approach them, you see their appearance changing, just as you discover new facets in the surrounding mountains and the lake, every hour, every day.

Many of the bunkers are situated in or on mounds. Sand flashes up their faces so they can be seen from a distance. Some are substantial in depth, but they are gently graded so that errant shots usually finish up in a spot that allows a play toward the hole. Fairway bunkers indicate the line of play and, at some holes, save errant shots from the woods.

The greens are well protected at the sides and backs by bunkers that tend to gather mishit approaches. Several holes feature bunkers that guard the front of the greens but are perhaps 20 or 30 yards short of the actual putting surfaces. This arrangement puts a premium on club selection on approaches, especially as the flashed faces make it appear

that the bunkers are tight to the greens. The greens have many subtle breaks and undulations, in addition to being steeply sloped from back to front in most cases.

The Jasper Park Lodge course is not particularly long, especially given the mountain setting, where the ball tends to carry farther than at sea level: 6,598 yards from the blues, 6,323 from the whites. Par is 71 as there are five par-threes. Thompson provided an excellent range of challenges for each kind of hole. Par-threes measure from 138 to 240 yards from the blues, from 120 to 220 from the whites; the par-fours include three in the 360-yard range and two at 454 and 468 respectively, from the blues. The par-fives range from a reachable 458 yards to a herculean 603. You will need every club in the bag here.

Many of the tees are elevated. The most exciting driving holes are Number 8, where you aim at a distant peak to try to place the ball between large mounds that guard both sides of the fairway; Number 14, a dogleg where the tee is situated on a small point and you cut off as much of the lake as you dare; Number 16 with its tight fairway guarded by water left

Greenside mounds at Jasper Park reflect the varying elevations of the distant mountain peaks.

Mountain streams and lakes join forces with Jasper Park's natural beauty to provide a scenic and sporting delight.

and trees right; and Number 18, a long, downhill dogleg with cavernous bunkers threatening every shot.

The 15th, called "The Bad Baby," is a superb par-three. It measures 138 yards from the blues, 120 from the whites, but it is a tantalizing target. The green is tiny, situated atop a mound with steep sides and a bunker left. Miss this green with your short-iron and you are assured of bogey or worse, especially if you have to pitch across the narrow putting surface. Thompson was unexcelled at designing par-threes.

The golf course is a gem and anyone with an interest in golf history or golf course architecture should find an opportunity to play this classic old course.

The accommodations at Jasper Park Lodge are on par with the course. The resort received the only gold medal awarded in Canada by the U.S. publication, GOLF, in 1989. The main lodge and surrounding cabins contain hundreds of rooms. The main building, built in the early 1950s, is beautiful, airy and peaceful. The floor is made of colorful flagstones; enormous picture windows look out to Lac Beauvert and the Whistlers; two huge fireplaces with hearths you could stand in are the focus of the sitting areas; massive beams and buttresses rise to the ceiling. The decor is tastefully done in every detail, both in the common areas and in the guest rooms. The cuisine and service are excellent and there is a myriad of activities for those few non-golfing hours.

In Love With Cleopatra

The single most memorable shot at Jasper Park Lodge is the tee shot at Number 9, "Cleopatra." A par-three that plays 231 yards from the blues, 214 from the whites, the tee is high on a hill, the green well below and heavily bunkered, sitting atop a mound with steep grassy sides. Choose your weapon, aim at a distant mountain top, and fire away: the drop from tee to green is so great that the ball seems to fly for minutes. The story is told that this hole derived its name as an offshoot of course architect Stanley Thompson's impish humor. Initially, as one stood on this tee, the voluptuous figure of Cleopatra became visible in the outlines of the fairway. Management of the Canadian National Railways, for whom Thompson built the course, persuaded him to disguise some of the contours, although the nickname stuck.

The appropriately named "Maze" is a short but convoluted par-five which starts off the back nine.

The mission at Kananaskis is to offer the green-fee player a private-club experience.

KANANASKIS

Country Golf Course

Architect: Robert Trent Jones
Director of Golf: Brian Bygrave
Head Professional: Wayne Bygrave
Superintendent: Jim O'Connor
Manager: Gord Sarkissian

No doubt, when Robert Trent Jones worked with revered Canadian course architect Stanley Thompson on his masterful layout at nearby Banff Springs, he dreamed of the time when he could tackle a similar challenge of his own in the awe-inspiring Rockies. He had to wait 50 years. His chance came in the early 1980s when the Alberta government decided to build a 72-hole golf facility in the Kananaskis River valley near Canmore, an hour west of Calgary.

The massive undertaking was funded by the Alberta Heritage Savings Trust Fund, staked by the province's huge oil production, and stands as a monument to both Jones and the foresight of the provincial government. Two courses, Mount Kidd and Mount Lorette, draw in the neighborhood of 75,000 golfers every season and it is safe to say that very few of that number are disappointed. They may echo Jones' sentiments when he first saw the proposed site: "the finest location I have ever seen for a golf course."

Despite their length — both layouts play to more than 7,000 yards from the tips — Jones provided four sets of tees to ensure that golfers of all abilities could enjoy his creations. Remember, as well, that the thin mountain air allows the ball to fly 10- to 15-per-cent further than at sea level; valuable input for club selection.

The par-three sixth hole on Mount Lorette — you will need a long-iron to a sharply sloping green protected by water.

All in all, Jones remained true to his design philosophy that each hole should be a tough par but an easy bogey.

Mount Kidd gives you little time to collect your wits before presenting what is rated the most difficult hole of its 18. The second hole is a par-five that stretches 536 yards from the white tees, usually into the wind. Take a moment on this tee to appreciate the green oasis that presents itself vividly against the grey granite backdrop of sheer mountain faces. Once back to reality, take care to avoid the righthand fairway bunkers with your tee shot and the river that edges up on the left as you approach the green. Four bunkers protect the relatively small green.

After negotiating the fourth hole, a par-three with a semi-island green that requires from a seven-iron to a four-iron with the wind at your back, you can start to anticipate the sixth. This challenging par-five is not overly long at 484 yards from the whites, but keeping the ball on the fairway is essential. The ideal landing spot is right, but that area is the location of a fairway bunker which complicates matters. A creek runs up the entire left side before looping behind the green and draining into a pond right of the putting surface. Dense forest guards the left boundary. The intelligent player will lay up in front of this tiered green.

Even taking the thin air into account, the finishing hole of Mount Kidd would make the longest hitters shudder. From the back tees, this hole is 642 yards, but the breathtaking scenery makes every moment spent here worthwhile. It has all the elements which characterize Kananaskis Country: dark-green forest, snow-capped mountains, shimmering water. Hit the tee shot as far as you can, bisect the fairway bunkers with a fairway wood on your second shot, place your mid- to short-iron approach on the right side of the pin, and you will be assured of a successful completion to your round.

Kananaskis Country Golf Course
Kananaskis Village, Alberta

Kidd	Length	Par	Rating
Gold	7049	72	74.5
Blue	6604	72	72
White	6068	72	69/74.5
Red	5539	72	66.5/71.5

Lorette	Length	Par	Rating
Gold	7102	72	74
Blue	6643	72	72
White	6155	72	69/76
Red	5429	72	64.5/72

Mount Kidd Course Hole	Yards	Par	Mount Lorette Course Hole	Yards	Par
1	455	4	1	412	4
2	615	5	2	416	4
3	437	4	3	395	4
4	197	3	4	254	3
5	339	4	5	541	5
6	553	5	6	195	3
7	415	4	7	482	4
8	183	3	8	408	4
9	408	4	9	560	5
OUT	3602	36	OUT	3663	36
10	405	4	10	402	4
11	355	4	11	497	5
12	183	3	12	394	4
13	392	4	13	407	4
14	491	5	14	523	5
15	402	4	15	188	3
16	207	3	16	380	4
17	370	4	17	185	3
18	642	5	18	463	4
IN	3447	36	IN	3439	36
Total	7049	72	Total	7102	72

Moving on to Mount Lorette, you have a slightly more hospitable welcome than at Mount Kidd. The Number 1 rated hole doesn't appear until the fifth tee. At 478 yards, this par-five doesn't test the player's length, but accuracy is a must. A small creek cuts in front of the tee and continues through trees on the left before looping around and embracing the green on three sides. The tee shot must avoid the left fairway bunkers and the brave second shot, if going for the narrow kidney-shaped green in two, should be a faded fairway wood. Be wary of the hidden pond right of the green. Those less confident, or more sensible, should plan to lay up and hope for par.

Many players consider the seventh hole, a 439-yard par-four when played from the blues, the best on the course. Your drive must carry a large pond and stay out of fairway traps which litter the middle and left of the landing area. Being right of these is a mixed blessing because the pond threatens that side. Those who are fortunate enough to avoid these hazards still must launch a long-iron into a well-bunkered, wavy green.

Touted as the most beautiful hole at Mount Lorette, the par-three 17th reminds the visitor why mountain golf in Canada is special. Lodge-pole pines direct your gaze at the mountains, and the Kananaskis River lies between tee and green, defined by three shimmering white sand traps.

The perfect outing at Kananaskis Country would be to play both courses in the same day, and it's not impossible because a round should not take longer than 4 1/2 hours. Golfers who complete 18 holes in less than that time are presented with a memento by the management. Kan-Alta Golf Management Ltd., which operates the facility under contract, promises to give public golfers a private-club experience and it's a credo they abide by.

Designer Robert Trent Jones called Kananaskis (opposite page) "the finest location I have ever seen for a golf course".

Ponoka, Alberta

WOLF CREEK

Golf Resort

Architect: Rod Whitman
Director of Golf: Ryan Vold
Superintendent: Rick David
Manager: Randy Dool

Wolf Creek is where Canada meets Scotland. Not geographically, of course, but where else would you find a links-style course that uses bleached cattle skulls for 150-yard markers?

Credit Ryan Vold and Rod Whitman with the audacity to dream up Wolf Creek and the perseverance to see it come to fruition in 1984. Vold, a member of the Canadian Professional Golfers' Association, saw the potential for a unique golf course on a portion of his family's ranch south of Edmonton. Conveniently, his friend Whitman had apprenticed under famed U.S. course architect Pete Dye. Whitman surveyed the dunes covered with waving native grasses and wildflowers and visualized a tribute to the origins of golf, set in the Canadian West.

Links-style holes, complete with unmaintained rough and enormous waste bunkers, make up a large part of the Wolf's character. Other holes are lined with trees and provide a contrast to the undulating dunes. Although the scorecard reveals a total length of less than 6,600 yards from the tips, Wolf Creek ravages less-than-competent players who dare to play from the back tees. The scorecard advises that only those with a handicap of five or less should attempt the full length, while those who carry a handicap of 16 or higher should step up to the whites.

As the site of the Canadian Tour's Alberta Open, the course has been the recipient of some glowing reviews. Tour Commissioner Bob Beauchemin heads the list when he sums up what his players thought of the course: "To a man, every player has mentioned what a fair, intriguing, difficult, challenging, fun course it is to play. And there are very few courses where you get that kind of unanimous opinion." Prominent Tour player Matt Cole of Windsor, Ontario, concurs: "You can't get nonchalant over one shot — not one drive, not one iron, not one putt." And veteran Canadian pro Bob Panasik harks back to the history of the game, saying, "This is my conception of how golf started. It's a unique golf course in our country."

You get the full impact of that uniqueness

The semi-island green on No. 4 is a real challenge. A ball hit to the back of the island is almost impossible to stop.

from the time you drive into the parking lot. A 20,000-square-foot solid log clubhouse is hunkered down against the wind that sweeps across the Prairies and plays havoc with delicate approach shots.

Wolf Creek spares no mercy for those who do not come prepared to play. "If you can get through the first four or five holes," says Vold, "you've got it made. Number 2 and four kill more people in tournaments than you can believe."

The opening hole is a dogleg-right with spruce trees guarding the lefthand side and massive mounds defining the right. If you hit the landing area, an eight- or nine-iron should get you to the heavily undulating green. Like many approaches at Wolf Creek, this shot can be played two ways: a bump-and-run during

Designer Rod Whitman used Alberta's natural contours to produce remarkable holes such as the par-five 11th.

Wolf Creek Golf Resort
Ponoka, Alberta

	Length	Par	Rating
Black	6548	70	74
Silver	5959	70/71	71/75
Blue	5786	70/71	70/74
White	4917	71	69

Hole	Yards	Par
1	391	4
2	393	4
3	199	3
4	385	4
5	410	4
6	533	5
7	133	3
8	344	4
9	445	4
OUT	3233	35
10	178	3
11	511	5
12	426	4
13	372	4
14	430	4
15	407	4
16	338	4
17	203	3
18	450	4
IN	3315	35
total	6548	70

dry weather, or a high short-iron during wet spells.

On Number 2, you must negotiate your tee shot through a tree-lined chute to a landing area 230 yards out from the back tees. The two-tiered green is protected by a sod-walled bunker directly in front. The third hole is a 199-yard par-three that requires anything from a one- to a six-iron depending on the ever-present wind. A very natural hole, again, lined with spruces with a green that runs right to left.

From the elevated tees of Hawk's Alley, the par-four fourth hole, use a three- or four-wood to blast the ball between black spruces. Wolf Creek, the body of water, defines the left boundary of the hole before coming back into play in a most dramatic way: it surrounds the semi-island green. "This is a very severe green," says Vold. "Drop down one club on your approach and run the ball onto the green. If you fly it into the green and hit the downslope on the back level, you just might find yourself in the pond."

Don't think just because you've survived the first four or five holes that your work at Wolf Creek is done. Number 9 has claimed some good golfers and Vold calls holes 11 through 13 "our Amen Corner," referring to the tough holes at Augusta National, site of The Masters tournament.

Buffalo Jump, the par-five 11th hole, is a dogleg-left with a creek running in front of the green. If you are 210 yards or less to the green on your second shot, go for it. Otherwise, lay up and appreciate the naturalness of Whitman's characteristic "potato-chip" greens which flow right into the natural surrounding mounds.

Touring pro Brad King was leading the 1988 Alberta Open when he came to Number 12. When he stepped off the green, he had dropped entirely from the leaderboard after carding a 12. "Any hole at Wolf Creek can do that to you," says Vold. "You have to keep your focus all the way around. Don't fall asleep or it will grab you." The 12th is relatively unprepossessing; the dogleg-left simply requires that you stay out of the woods. Of course, there is a slight matter, hardly worth mentioning, of why they call this hole The Gorge. You must carry this ravine about 175 yards out to reach

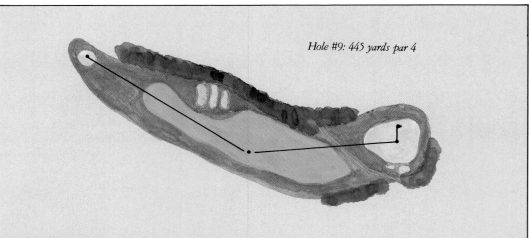

Hole #9: 445 yards par 4

A Heap of Trouble

The ninth hole at Wolf Creek may rank as only the third-toughest handicap hole on the course, but to at least a couple of Canadian Tour pros, there is no doubt it should be Number 1. During the 1990 Alberta Open, the 445-yard par-four claimed two victims in outrageous fashion. The hole calls for a long drive followed by a second shot over a ravine that features a creek and trees on either side. The green is not noted for being receptive to anything but a perfect approach. Toronto's Jack Kay Jr., a young pro with great talent who has played on the U.S. PGA Tour, thought he had it all together as he stepped onto the ninth tee. Twelve shots later, his ball collapsed with relief into the hole. One of Kay's compatriots, whose identity we are sworn not to reveal, took 14 whacks to complete this hole. He walked from the ninth green directly to his car, drove away and never looked back.

the landing area. Hit a fairway wood to the right side of the fairway.

The 13th hole completes this stretch. A drive to the upper deck on this dogleg-left leaves you only a short-iron into a flat green, half of which is hidden behind a steep-walled bunker.

Another nine holes, designed by Whitman in a similar, though even more natural, style were completed in 1990.

You must clear "The Gorge" on your way to parring the par-four 12th.

Often called one of the world's most scenic courses, Capilano sits high above the port city of Vancouver.

West Vancouver, British Columbia

CAPILANO

Golf and Country Club

Architect: Stanley Thompson
Head Professional: Gerry Chatelain
Manager: Greg Hartigan
Superintendent: David Sullivan

Understandably, many first-time visitors to Capilano find it hard to concentrate on playing one of Stanley Thompson's finest creations because they are so awed by its spectacular setting. Capilano Golf and Country Club, nestled in the mountains overlooking the beautiful harbor city of Vancouver, is no doubt the most scenic golf course in this country, and must be in the Top 10 in the world in that category. But those novices will soon realize that the demands the course makes on their visual senses will be equalled by the demands on their golfing abilities.

"Visually, it's a gorgeous course," says PGA Tour pro Jim Nelford, who grew up on the West Coast and who has played around the world. "The course is cut right out of the forest. It's away from the city, above the smog. When you get on the first tee, you get a view of all of Vancouver. You just look down the hill and the city is laid out in front of you. And then when you're through playing, it's a real pleasure to go into the clubhouse, which is a grand old thing that sits way on top of everything. You can see the last five holes from the clubhouse, as well as the first hole and the 13th green. What a breathtaking view from up there. Capilano is an old course with plenty of class. . . . One of the best courses I've ever played."

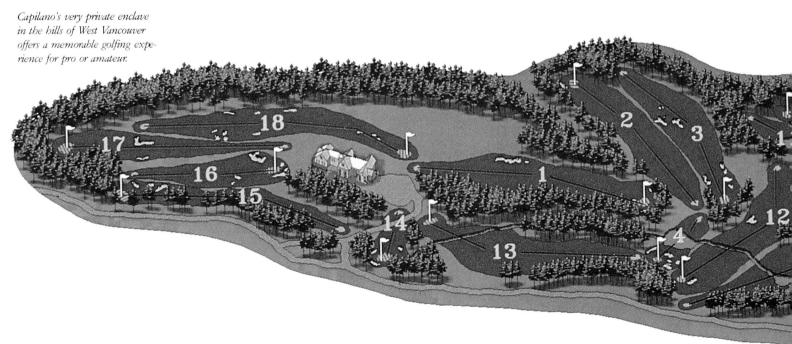

Capilano's very private enclave in the hills of West Vancouver offers a memorable golfing experience for pro or amateur.

This unparalleled experience grew from the vision and determination of A.J.T. Taylor, an investment broker who was born on Vancouver Island in 1887, and is indelibly linked with the development of West Vancouver itself. Taylor negotiated the purchase of 6,000 acres (at $20 an acre) across the inlet from Vancouver, offering wealthy Britons a land development opportunity. The area, still known as the British Properties and one of the most prestigious locales in the region, at the time was linked with Vancouver only by slow, unreliable ferries. Taylor, using the financial clout of the Guinness Brewing Co., a major investor in the British Properties, bullied through the building of a bridge to the city. The Lions Gate Bridge cost $5.7 million and was the second-longest suspension bridge in the world at the time, trailing only San Francisco's Golden Gate Bridge.

Auspiciously, the bridge was opened by King George VI in 1939, the same year as the clubhouse at Capilano Golf and Country Club, the jewel in the British Properties crown. Seven years earlier, Taylor had enlisted the outstanding Canadian course architect Stanley Thompson to design a layout on Hollyburn Mountain west of the Capilano River. (Thompson received less than $7,000, including fees, plans and expenses, for his labors.)

"We feel hopeful that this project may prove our best endeavor on this continent," says Thompson in correspondence to the course developers. Considering Thompson's body of work, that was a tall, but prophetic, statement. That the course has remained largely unchanged from that original design is testimony to Thompson's abilities and a tribute to an intelligent membership with a continuing deep understanding of the game.

Jock McKinnon, who was the revered head professional here for 42 years, put it this way: "Capilano was and still is a tribute to the architectural genius of Stanley Thompson. There is no need for any tampering apart from taking care of the normal wear and tear. The members have a work of art in their care and possession. My advice is that they should never permit this to be spoiled by people who come along as they have done, and will, and suggest changes at great cost in what I think is a useless attempt to improve a great golf course."

Capilano has had an illustrious membership. In 1937, one year after the course opened, the country's top-ranked amateur arrived and and stayed to make an indelible impression on the club's stately and sensible development. Ken Black, then 26 years old, won the 1939 Canadian Amateur and was made one of the club's first honorary members. He did not play in another national championship until 1946 (the tournament was suspended during the war years) and, much like another famed amateur, Bobby Jones, retired from competitive golf prematurely. Only 34, he became very active in club affairs and is regarded as a guiding

Capilano Golf and Country Club
West Vancouver, British Columbia

	Length	Par	Rating
Blue	6578	72	72
White	6274	72	70
Yellow	5964	74	74

Hole	Yards	Par
1	482	5
2	400	4
3	467	5
4	172	3
5	520	5
6	394	4
7	426	4
8	381	4
9	176	3
OUT	3418	37
10	434	5
11	165	3
12	368	4
13	400	4
14	130	3
15	430	4
16	247	3
17	425	4
18	557	5
IN	3156	35
Total	6574	72

Towering evergreens line Capilano's fairways and make accuracy a must.

light. Other members have claimed national titles and Capilano has played host to innumerable tournaments at all levels.

The club has also been a gracious host to an international who's who, ranging from Bob Hope, Bing Crosby and Billy Graham, to heads of state such as the prime ministers of Japan and Malaysia. In 1971, the clubhouse was the site of a notable wedding reception, that of Pierre and Margaret Trudeau.

"Apart from its natural beauty, this is an ideal golf course," says former Masters champion George Archer, now a standout on the Seniors Tour, "because it is a fair test for the members from the middle tees, and is easily transformed into an excellent championship course from the back tees without tricking up the greens or the rough or the approaches."

To get the best from your round at Capilano, "get your birdies early," says Head Professional Gerry Chatelain. There are three reachable par-fives in the first five holes here, offering an opportunity to gain a couple of strokes from par. The test may come right after those five holes, on the relatively undemanding sixth hole. This short par-four, a drive and a wedge

for most players, has proved to be the most difficult hole in many of the tournaments played here, says Chatelain. To get your four, hit an iron off the tee into the narrow landing area; above all, don't miss the fairway.

Holes seven and eight also claim their share of victims. On the seventh, the Number 1 stroke hole at Capilano, a drive into a gully leaves you with any combination of uneven lies. From there, you hit through a very narrow entrance to a difficult green. Number 8 shares some characteristics with the preceding hole: a shortish par-four with a well-protected green, and a predilection for bogeys.

Once you reach the final four holes, you may regret not having heeded Chatelain's advice about concentrating on those early birdie chances. Capilano's strong finishing holes start at the dogleg-left, par-four 15th, which is followed by a 250-yard par-three. The 17th hole is another strong par-four. The final hole is a tough par-five that features a blind shot into the largest green on the golf course, meaning the emphasis is on correct club selection. The green is on a plateau and protected by bunkers.

Jock McKinnon's Eclectic Record

Jock McKinnon, Capilano's head pro for 42 years, was a fine player in his own right. He is in the record book, however, for a golfing feat that may never be equalled: an eclectic score of 33, recognized by the Guinness Book of World Records. An eclectic score is the sum of a player's all-time personal low scores for each hole on one course, and McKinnon's record is 33, accomplished over 21 years. His eclectic scorecard looks like this:

$$222 \ 122 \ 221 — 16$$
$$212 \ 212 \ 223 — 17$$

This astounding 39-under-par figure consists of four double-eagles, 18 eagles and one birdie. In Eric Whitehead's excellent book on Capilano, "Hathstauwk", it is noted that McKinnon started this streak during the first round he ever played on the course, just a few weeks after his arrival from Scotland in 1937.

The finishing holes at Capilano have represented the turning point in many tournaments.

Tucked amid sand hills and gullies in central British Columbia, Gallaghers Canyon is a long and difficult test.

GALLAGHERS CANYON

Golf Resort

Architect: Bill Robinson
Managing Director: Dick Munn
Head Professional: Rick Montgomery
Superintendent: Ashley LeGeyt

The Okanagan region of south-central British Columbia has many attributes: exceptional orchards, a mythical monster which allegedly dwells in Lake Okanagan, and one of the most moderate climates in the country. It can also claim some of the best courses in Canada, including Gallaghers Canyon.

The story of Gallaghers Canyon is phoenix-like, arising as it does from the ashes of another's failure. The incredibly rugged terrain overlooking two canyons, Gallaghers and Scenic, was initially seen as a golf course by a Kelowna-based developer who, before running into financial troubles, had the good sense to hire Bill Robinson of White Rock, British Columbia.

"I was working at the Point Grey club in Vancouver at the time," says Managing Director Dick Munn, a Canadian PGA professional. "Bill Robinson was doing some work there and told me there was no way this great course near Kelowna was going to get built, because of a lack of financing. I didn't think too much about it, but the very next day, my mother called to say she needed a ride — to Kelowna! So, I thought, 'Hmm, Kelowna twice in two days. Maybe I'd better have a look.'"

Munn didn't have to look twice. With the financial backing of

The par-four opening hole at
Gallaghers Canyon.

Gallaghers Canyon Golf Resort
Kelowna, British Columbia

	Length	Par	Rating
Gold	6975	72	74
Black	6494	72	71
Silver	5604	72	69

Hole	Yards	Par
1	434	4
2	331	4
3	367	4
4	360	4
5	178	3
6	425	4
7	420	4
8	345	4
9	589	5
OUT	3449	36
10	596	5
11	414	4
12	550	5
13	187	3
14	443	4
15	350	4
16	218	3
17	409	4
18	359	4
IN	3526	36
Total	6975	72

longtime friend Angus Mackenzie, a Calgary oilman, he acquired the property. The course opened in 1980 to rave reviews, as much for its fantastic setting as for its fine layout. The course overlooks a spine-chilling ravine that cuts through massive sand hills and dunes, creating unmatched vistas from many vantage points.

One thing you won't see is the "resort" part of Gallaghers Canyon Golf Resort. Priorities have changed in the years since it was named in 1980, as has ownership of the property. The surrounding acreage has been zoned for residential development, so Munn and his partners decided to cash in on that favorable decision. They sold the course in 1990 to Burrard International, which is involved in development in California and British Columbia. Munn continues to stay involved in Gallaghers and other projects.

"I've been in the golf business for many years," says Munn, "and I can say honestly that I've never been at a place where so many people come to say how much they enjoyed themselves." Munn used that experience, gained at Banff and Tucson National in Arizona, to come up with his philosophy of serving the golfing public. "We like to say that a great golf course is a total experience, and we try to be as conscientious as possible to ensure our golfers get that experience."

Gallaghers has a well-deserved reputation as one of the tougher tracks in the country.

When the Canadian Amateur was played here in 1988, only one player, eventual winner Doug Roxburgh of Vancouver, finished under-par. But Munn says the course could be tougher, and better, but continues to suffer from construction deficiencies encountered during the transition of ownership back in 1980. "It had the potential to be one of the greatest courses ever," Munn says wistfully. "I wish we had been here right from the beginning." An ongoing upgrading program ensures that the course will continue to improve, and become even more difficult.

"There is no stretch of gimme holes here, just as there isn't a stretch of killer holes," asserts Munn. That assertion may be hard to swallow when you are standing on the highly elevated first tee (built on top of the cart storage facility), under the direct gaze of every eye in the clubhouse. More than 430 yards away awaits the elevated green. All you have to do is steer the ball between two lines of Ponderosa pines that delineate the edges of the fairway. Ignore the dozens of gophers scurrying around, all the while trying not to feel like Bill Murray in the movie Caddyshack, and swing easy. You're on your way.

The front nine concludes with its only par-five, but it is worth the wait. At almost 600 yards from the back tee, you will appreciate the fact that the elevation here adds some distance to your swing, but don't abuse that

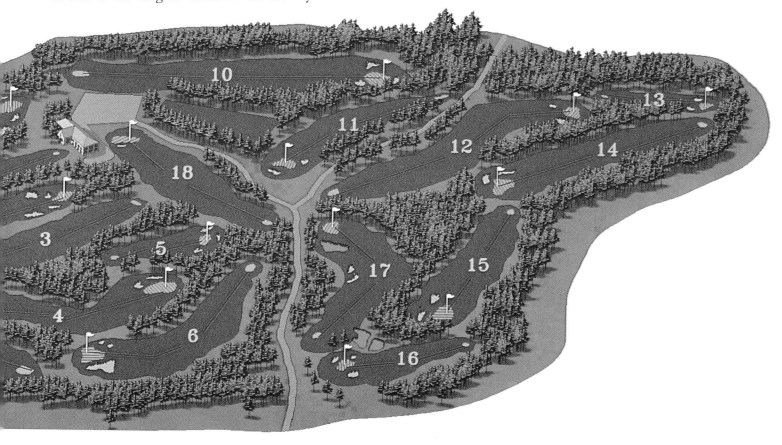

privilege by over-swinging. An enormous gulch cuts into the left boundary of this hole and a hooked shot is history. Only the longest hitters will contemplate trying to reach this sloped green in two.

The 12th hole is a joy to play, despite the fact that it is described as a narrow, double-dogleg par-five of some 550 yards from the back tees. Keep the ball in the fairway and a pleasant surprise awaits in what is, in Gal-laghers Canyon terms, a sympathetic green. High-handicappers are advised to lay up on their second shot into the par-four 17th hole. Try to knock your third shot close to the pin on this well-mounded, long and narrow putting surface.

The finishing hole is a tempting par-four of only 350 yards that uses a single tree in the fairway to give you a line off the tee. A fade to the right of the tree is best, but if

The Toughest Hole at Gallaghers Canyon

The par-four sixth hole is Gallaghers Canyon in microcosm: trees, slopes, elevated green and so on. It plays 425 yards from the back tees, 403 from the black and 400 from the silver. No matter what tee is used, the hole reeks of trouble. The left side of the landing area slopes down to a very steep embankment while a shot crowding the right side is blocked off by a grove of spindly pines. Emphasis is on a straight tee shot to avoid kicking into the rough or trees. That elevated green is tucked back and away in a corner surrounded by sand and trees.

you don't want to risk being behind it, use a three-iron. Your short-iron approach is to another elevated green which slopes toward the fairway.

"At Gallaghers, you must use all the clubs in your bag and try not to be distracted by the scenery, the views, the vistas," Munn advises. "What can make or break your round is your attitude, strangely enough. You can't try to force your way around this golf course. You might use your driver five or six times in a round. Peter Thomson (five-time British Open champion and course architect of note) visited here regularly and used his driver five times a round at most. Just resign yourself to take what the golf course gives you."

Almost 600 yards from the back tees, No. 9 is a true three-shot hole.

A delight to play, Royal Colwood is a golfing jewel on Vancouver Island.

———— *Victoria, British Columbia* ————

ROYAL COLWOOD

Golf Club

Architect: A.V. Macan
Head Professional: Bob Hogarth
Manager: Bruce Craigie
Superintendent: Geoff Bunting

Tucked in behind some of the most impressive Douglas firs and oaks found in arboreal British Columbia is another of Canada's "royal" courses — Royal Colwood Golf Club. Although a busy shopping and residential community has grown up around Royal Colwood since it was built on Goldstream Road back in 1913, these dignified sentinels maintain the serenity that has always typified the club.

Indeed, surviving depictions of the two men — Joseph Sayward and James Dunsmuir — reveal the essence of a pair of solemn, wealthy gentlemen. Sayward, a stout lumber baron with a flowing walrus moustache, was "known to be grumpy three or four times a day," a club history notes. Dunsmuir served as premier and later lieutenant-governor of British Columbia. The two, concerned about the encroachment of the city on Victoria Golf Club, then the pre-eminent club in the region, purchased 240 acres of farmland outside of the city for $183,722 in 1912. Then they approached the most prominent course designer in the Pacific Northwest, A. Vernon Macan.

"Mac" Macan, an Irish lawyer who settled in British Columbia in 1910, had a reputation as one of the finest amateur golfers

The par-four 17th hole.

Royal Status Attained

How the Colwood Golf Club eventually joined the ranks of the other "royal" clubs in Canada (the others are Royal Ottawa, Royal Quebec and Royal Montreal, all in the province of Quebec), is slightly confusing, according to a history of the club prepared for its 75th anniversary in 1988. The Prince of Wales (later King Edward VIII and, upon his abdication, the Duke of Windsor), had played golf several times at Colwood while visiting the Dunsmuirs at their estate, Hatley Park. He consented to become a patron of the club and, on July 29, 1931, permission was given by his father, King George V, to change the name to Royal Colwood Golf Club. For some reason still unclear, the designation was retracted shortly thereafter. One theory is that the Victoria Golf Club had applied for the designation in 1910, but the request was not acted upon. In any case, a communication from the king, dated five years after the initial decision, now hangs in Royal Colwood's clubhouse, confirming the club's enviable status.

in the region. He promptly won the B.C. Amateur Championship in 1912 and soon turned his hand to golf course architecture. His competitive fervor was reflected in his design principles: he built the exquisitely difficult Shaughnessy Golf and Country Club in Vancouver, among others. But Macan would always point with pride at Royal Colwood, identifying holes 11, 12 and 13 as his masterpieces. "All par-fours should require two well-planned and -played shots to the green," he said once when asked about his guidelines. "And greens should not be flat, but hogbacks, undulations and crowns should be incorporated to defy the backspin players." Macan must have been a formidable opponent in either match-play or arguments over hole design. Even after losing a leg below the knee in the First World War, he continued to play to a four handicap.

His task at Royal Colwood was aided by the natural beauty of the property. Some majestic trees already were in place and others have been added; all have flourished under the gentle climate of Vancouver Island. In addition, the land was largely rich, black loam and water was readily available. The resulting layout, which has been largely adhered to in the intervening 80 years was as expected — visually impressive and daunting to even the finest players.

Two famous players, Bobby Locke of South Africa and Canadian Ken Black, shared the competitive course record of three-under-par 67 for almost 30 years, despite Royal Colwood playing host to numerous provincial, regional and national championships including the Canadian Amateur in 1967 and 1976. Jim Hallett broke that mark with a stunning 63 at the 1985 Victoria Open. The low ladies' score, set by Marlene Stewart Streit in 1955, is 70. Senior PGA Tour star Bruce Crampton has said Royal Colwood is as close to perfection as possible, and veteran Tour player Frank Beard calls it one of the 10 best courses in the world.

Every year, due in large part to the balmy temperatures year-round in Victoria, some 90,000 rounds are played at Royal Colwood. (In view of this amount of play, the greens staff ought to be knighted for the pristine conditioning of the course.) There is no question that Colwood's ethereal surroundings, created by the towering trees and typified by the 16th hole, "Cathedral," reward each of the 90,000 with a memorable golfing experience. To complete that experience, however, they must cope with the course's challenging layout, tall rough, narrow fairways and those characteristically tricky Macan-designed greens.

Cathedral, so named by the Prince of Wales, is "encased in giant heritage fir trees," says eloquent Head Professional Bob Hogarth. The 380-yard par-four requires a positioned tee shot and then a short-iron over front bunkers. Remember that this is the Pacific Northwest and there will be little roll on fairways and

*Solemn firs line the "Cathedral"
— the 16th hole.*

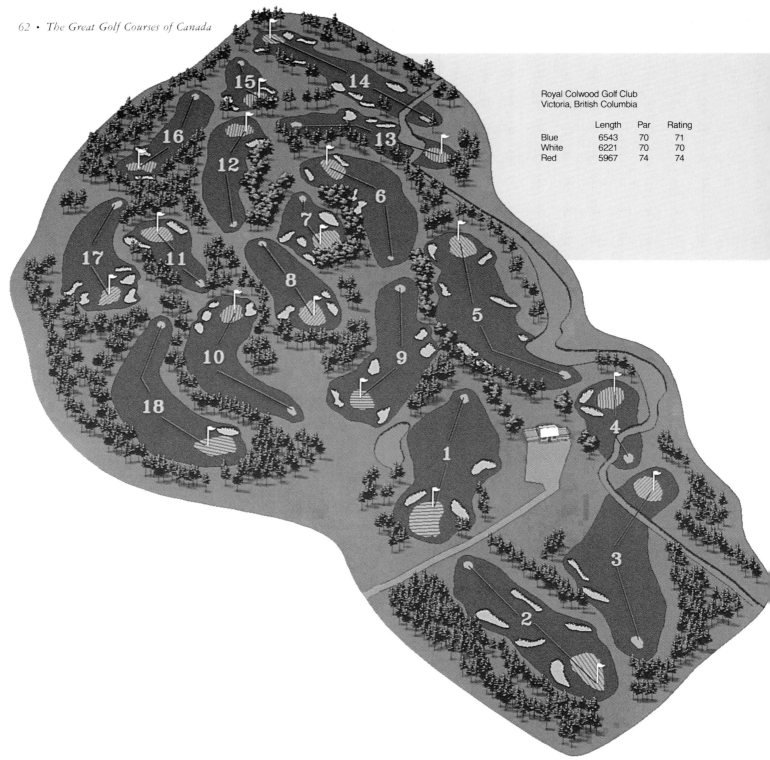

Royal Colwood Golf Club
Victoria, British Columbia

	Length	Par	Rating
Blue	6543	70	71
White	6221	70	70
Red	5967	74	74

greens softened by regular rainfall. Hit your approaches at Royal Colwood as close to the pin as possible to avoid long putts over these sneaky-quick greens with their trademark undulations.

The essence of Royal Colwood is distilled on the third hole, rated the toughest on the course. With out-of-bounds on the right, and two fairway bunkers on the left, this long dogleg-right demands a true tee shot. After placing your drive as close to the bunkers as possible, a long-iron is called for into a gently sloping green guarded by trees and water.

The course features only two par-fives, thus

the par of 70. The first encountered is the 513-yard fifth hole. This hole is a dogleg-right with a stand of fir trees on the right side of the fairway. Hogarth says a large oak tree about 350 yards out could close out a straight drive. In order to reach this green in two, you must hit the long fade off the tee. Any approach must respect the rolling, well-trapped green. The 14th hole is shorter at 482 yards, but out-of-bounds right and trees left define the landing area. "Tee it high and let it fly," advises the pro, saying that the drive is key to this hole. The green is bunkered left and right but open in front.

Hole	Yards	Par			
1	398	4	10	427	4
2	405	4	11	241	3
3	426	4	12	423	4
4	152	3	13	386	4
5	513	5	14	494	5
6	432	4	15	160	3
7	168	3	16	387	4
8	327	4	17	396	4
9	405	4	18	403	4
OUT	3226	35	IN	3317	35
			Total	6543	70

At 241 yards from the back tees, the par-three 11th is a huge challenge.

———— *Vancouver, British Columbia* ————

SHAUGHNESSY

Golf and Country Club

Architect: A.V. Macan
Manager: Ron Kleinschmidt
Superintendent: Brian Houston

The history of Shaughnessy Golf and Country Club, as is the case with many older clubs in Canada, begins in the early part of this century at a location other than where the present course now stands. Shaughnessy's history spans two different sites and a remarkable four clubhouses — but only five head professionals in 80 years.

The club is steeped in tradition, dating back to 1911 when nine affluent businessmen, in co-operation with Canadian Pacific Railways, founded the Shaughnessy Heights Golf Club, in what now is downtown Vancouver. The first nine holes opened in 1912 and Shaughnessy's position as the sporting citadel of Vancouver was established. In 1947, the CPR advised the club that it would not extend the lease on the land beyond 1960 and the search for new quarters began.

After a lengthy process, a 160-acre parcel on the University of British Columbia's endowment lands, owned by the Musqueam Indians, was selected and a lease running until 2032 was arranged. When the new club opened in 1961 — with the name revised to Shaughnessy Golf and Country Club — Canadian architect A.V. Macan had built "the toughest golf course possible," says Director

The eighth hole is the longest par-three: 180 yards.

of Golf Jack McLaughlin. As evidence, the winning score in the 1966 Canadian Open played here was a four-under-par 280 by Don Massengale of Texas.

The tradition at Shaughnessy is matched by the physical beauty of its setting on the bank of the mighty Fraser River. Insulated from the few surrounding homes by towering evergreens and hardwoods, Shaughnessy stands in the shadow of snow-capped mountains that provide not only an esthetic marvel, but protect the course well from wind. In the spring, blossoms are draped from the multitude of cherry and dogwood trees. And the pleasure of playing this course can be enjoyed almost year-round. The one day of the year it is sure to be closed is Christmas, but it has never

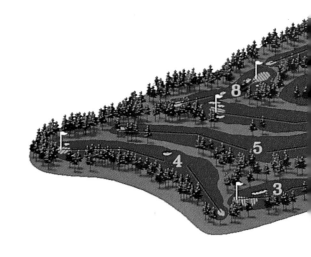

been out of play for more than 41 days during any year in its history.

The continuing efforts of local architect Norman Woods and others to make Shaughnessy more palatable to mid- and high-handicap members have softened the course considerably, but without loss of continuity or challenge. Many of Macan's original "inverted saucer" greens which permitted only the most delicate run-up shots to stay on their surface have been rebuilt. As well, Shaughnessy remains the only course of its calibre in the area with sufficient length for a major championship, and it has played host to many. Ongoing renovations to bunkers throughout the course have been carried out by Les Furber of Canmore, Alberta. The club is pondering a radical change to the fifth hole, at present a short par-five, to make it an outstanding par-four which would become Shaughnessy's "signature" hole.

Scoring well here means playing the nine par-fours brilliantly. Length off the tee is vital because, due to Vancouver's moist climate, the fairways are generally soft and roll is minimal. Accuracy is also a must because that same benevolent climate ensures that the rough is long and lush and the layout is dotted with bunkers. Huge trees line most fairways, making it easy to believe the course has been here since time immemorial. Try to appreciate the firs and maples from the fairway since advancing the ball from among them can be an onerous task.

Of the par-fours, the fourth hole is the toughest on the course and plays 400 yards from the members' tees. A sharp dogleg-left challenges the player to hit a high draw and then fire a mid-iron into a green that falls away quickly. On Number 6, a left-to-right tee shot will leave you only a short iron into an elevated green. Some members rate the 407-yard 10th hole as the most demanding par-four. Standing back in a chute, you must keep your tee shot between two narrow stands of trees while avoiding the Fraser River on the left. The second shot is hit down to the green, making stopping the ball a test. Fortunately,

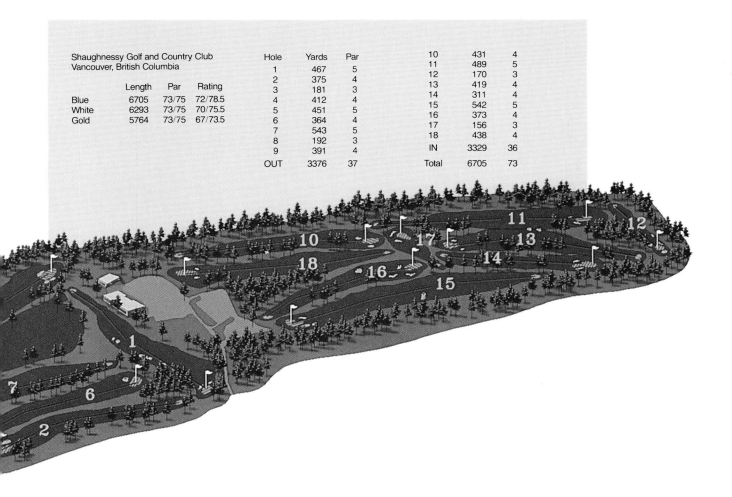

Shaughnessy Golf and Country Club Vancouver, British Columbia				Hole	Yards	Par			
				1	467	5	10	431	4
				2	375	4	11	489	5
	Length	Par	Rating	3	181	3	12	170	3
				4	412	4	13	419	4
Blue	6705	73/75	72/78.5	5	451	5	14	311	4
White	6293	73/75	70/75.5	6	364	4	15	542	5
Gold	5764	73/75	67/73.5	7	543	5	16	373	4
				8	192	3	17	156	3
				9	391	4	18	438	4
				OUT	3376	37	IN	3329	36
							Total	6705	73

Canadian architect Les Furber has renovated all of the bunkers on A.V. Macan's original layout.

again due to the amount of rainfall, the greens generally hold very well. The 13th is the Number 2 rated hole at Shaughnessy and plays every one of its 405 yards, especially if the east wind is up. Hit your drive long and close to the right rough and a four-iron should get you home, but remember it is all carry, so take enough club.

The five par-fives are not unreachable by most players, with the possible exception of Number 15. The opening hole is less than 500 yards, but a bogey can result if you get too aggressive and try to carry the trees on the left of this double-dogleg. The aforementioned fifth can be reached in two, but remember that the railway ties marking the pond in front of the green are on the fairway side of the water. If redesigned to incorporate an island green, this would make a wonderful par-four and reduce Shaughnessy's par to a more conventional 72. The longest hole on the course is the 15th at 518 yards from the members' tees and 542 from the back. Accept that it

is the only legitimate three-shotter at Shaughnessy and lay up in front of the well-bunkered green that slopes back-to-front.

The four par-threes are attractive, though most are short. The 180-yard eighth hole is the longest and could require as much as a two-iron, depending on conditions. The unusual green site on 17, sloping front-to-back, makes club selection more of a priority than usual.

The 18th, another fine par-four, brings you back to Shaughnessy's clubhouse. This sprawling cedar structure, dotted with skylights and surrounded by lovely displays of flowers and shrubbery, reminds you that this is the West Coast, and you have just played one of the finest layouts here or anywhere in Canada.

On a sad note, I just learned that my good friend Jack McLaughlin, head pro at Shaughnessy recently passed away in Palm Springs, California. He died doing what he loved best, playing golf.

Tradition is Everything

When Shaughnessy Heights Golf Club opened, W. Bowden received the sum of $75 a month to serve as its first head professional. Since he assumed his duties in 1912, the club has had only five professionals. Alfred Blinko replaced Bowden in 1913, staying until 1920, the year Davie Black was hired. Black, a native of Scotland, was an outstanding player, winning the Canadian PGA Championship four times. His retirement in 1945 opened the door for Fred Wood, who stepped down in 1972. After a brief stay by Len Collett, present head pro Jack McLaughlin took over. McLaughlin, a renowned instructor, is a worthy successor to the likes of Davie Black. His pupils, including PGA Tour player Ray Stewart, continue to make their mark on amateur and professional events worldwide. McLaughlin is also credited with founding the Junior-Junior program, an innovative plan to develop young golfers which is being introduced across Canada.

Just over 300 yards long, the par-four 14th hole is a birdie chance.

VICTORIA

Golf Club

Architect: A. V. Macan
Head Professional: Mike Parker
Manager: Don Francis
Superintendent: Alec Kazai

If you've heard rumors of a fantastic, mysterious golf links on Vancouver Island called Oak Bay, this is it. It has been officially known as the Victoria Golf Club since 1893, the year a band of hardy hackers rented farmland surrounded on two sides by the ocean and proceeded to lay out 11 holes. The club is the oldest in the Pacific Northwest still in existence, followed by the Tacoma Club (1894) in the neighboring state of Washington.

In his book, A Guide to the Golf Courses of British Columbia, Alan Dawe says, "Tradition has it that members of the Victoria Golf Club eventually had to buy this property because the farmers they leased it from had the unfortunate habit of driving all golfers off the fairways during the summer months so that their cows and sheep could safely graze."

If true, then that was the last time that anyone or anything forced the membership off

its links. Fiercely proud of its reputation as "the" golf club on Vancouver Island, this very private establishment is equally proud of its course — and justifiably so.

However, says Head Professional Mike Parker, if anything could push a golfer off this layout, it would be the wind. "You're right on the ocean and the wind is very much a factor," says Parker. The back tee for the par-three ninth hole is on a postage-stamp of land leaning into the ocean and new members are baptized by the spray crashing over the tee. "Sometimes you have to have someone hold your ball on the tee," says the pro, "otherwise it will blow off. Timing is very important on this shot!" On the preceding hole, a 115-yarder, Parker has hit a wedge on still days — and a hard three-iron when faced with a winter gale. Facing a winter gale is not unusual at the Victoria Golf Club. Parker says the course is open more days than any other in Canada, due to the moderate climate of southern Vancouver Island which allows golfing year-round.

Those foolish enough to write off this course as a pushover because the card reveals a length from the back tees of just over 6,000 yards are in for a rude awakening. Since positioning is vital on this narrow, devious design routed through just 97 rolling acres, it may be wise to give the driver a day off. Irons from the tee are the rule here with only a few exceptions, a situation that makes the golf course seem longer. In addition, a modern irrigation system tends to prevent any significant roll. "In large part," says Parker, "the irrigation has taken away a lot of the bump-and-run aspect of this course. Now players can fly the ball into the greens and they will hold the shot. I know players who say they used to drive the 18th

At only 145 yards, the second hole rates the nickname "Calamity."

Victoria Golf Club
Victoria, British Columbia

	Length	Par	Rating
Blue	6015	70	69
White	5857	71	68

Hole	Yards	Par
1	502	5
2	145	3
3	402	4
4	362	4
5	324	4
6	341	4
7	369	4
8	115	3
9	194	3
OUT	2754	34
10	350	4
11	438	5
12	521	5
13	158	3
14	194	3
15	404	4
16	356	4
17	450	5
18	390	4
IN	3261	37
Total	6015	71

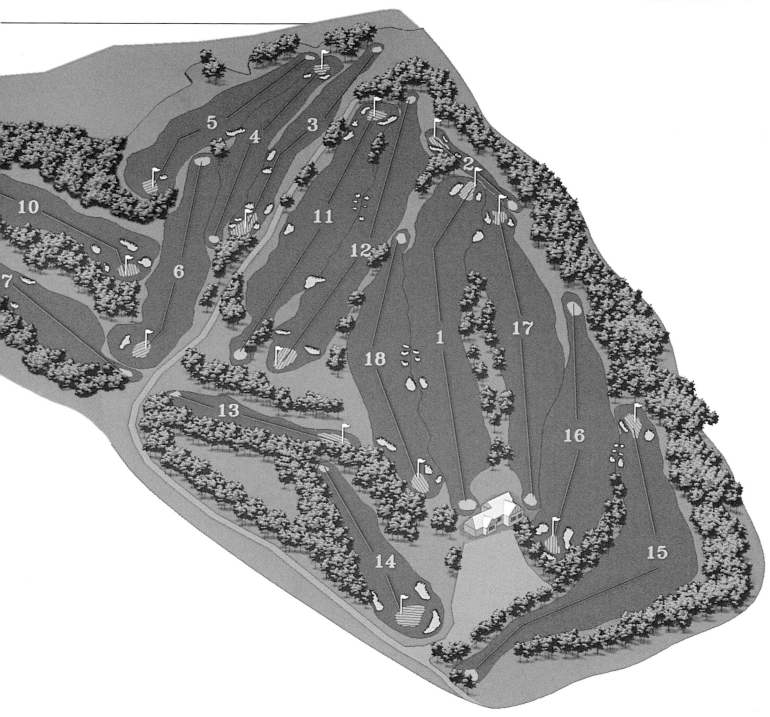

green (390 yards) in the days before irrigation, when the fairways were hard and fast. Now if you're within a hundred yards of the green, you're a hero."

Parker says the first two holes at Victoria Golf Club are reasonable warm-ups, even though the first hole is a 500-yard par-five into that notorious wind. The third hole is rated the toughest on the course and a hint of what's to come is found in its name: the Road Hole. Like its excruciatingly difficult namesake at the Old Course at St. Andrews in Scotland, a roadway figures in the layout.

But in this case, the road is Beach Drive, which trails along the left boundary of the hole. The fairway is not wide, but downwind, fortunately. Use a driver or three-wood off the tee and you will be left with a mid-iron into a three-level green that is 40 yards deep. Obviously, there is some anxiety involved in club selection for that second shot.

Once on the green, there is still much work to be done, for Victoria is touted to have the fastest greens in the West. In general, they are not large, although they do vary in size. They are characterized by undulations that are

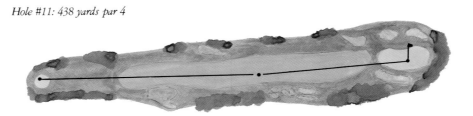

Hole #11: 438 yards par 4

The Toughest Hole at Victoria

Though it's rated the Number 2 stroke hole, Head Professional Mike Parker calls the 11th hole at the Victoria Golf Club the most difficult on the course. It's a 438-yard par-four from the blue tees (a 458-yard par-five from the whites) and epitomizes the course's emphasis on positioning and pinpoint accuracy. "You have to play this into the wind and there's out-of-bounds all down the left side. Take a long-iron off the tee and you've still got a very difficult second shot. If you hit two good ones, you deserve to make par, and the green reflects that because it's one of the most level surfaces on the golf course."

Victoria's seaside setting contributes to its "links" atmosphere.

No. 5 is a short but exquisitely beautiful par-four.

reminiscent of the waves crashing into the nearby shore. Instead of swales, tiers and humps, one thinks of the greens as possessing breakers, combers, rollers and chutes; the putting surfaces are that idiosyncratic. "There are very few flat lies," confirms Parker. "We find it compensates for the length." Without a doubt.

The fifth hole, appropriately called The Bay, is a shortish par-four notable for two things: a very quick green even by Victoria Golf Club standards, and the start of a spectacular stretch of holes parallel to the ocean. The next hole, Vimy Ridge, forces the player to hit a blind tee shot over the ridge onto a plateau. From there, he must hit another blind shot to a green some 10 metres below the level of the fairway. "A members' hole," concedes Parker.

If you don't feel up to playing the seventh hole as a par-four, you have the option of playing it as the par-three it used to be, thanks to some novel course renovations several years ago. The ocean comes into play on the left from the tee all the way to a very severe green.

The back nine provides no respite. Hit a one- or two-iron off the tee of the 350-yard 10th hole and, if you can battle the left-to-right sloping fairway and the wind which pushes the ball right, then you will have anything from a six-iron to a wedge in. Number 12 is the first of two par-fives on the back nine. The three-level green is severely trapped with pot bunkers and mounding, making it advisable to lay up on the second shot and try to knock your third tight to the pin position of the day.

The 13th and 14th holes are par-threes, but the latter is superior, especially from the back tee which is elevated. You have no option but to hit to the green that slopes away from you — there is no fairway, and out-of-bounds lurks left, right and over the green. Your trials continue until the 17th, which Parker admits is a "members' par-five." A birdie opportunity is treasured at Victoria.

—— *Whistler Village, British Columbia* ——

WHISTLER

Golf Club

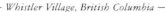

Architect: Arnold Palmer
Head Professional: Scott Staley
Superintendent: Dave Gottselig

After the white-knuckled, two-hour drive up the spectacular Squamish Highway from Vancouver into the mountains that surround Whistler Village, anticipating an anti-climax would be understandable. But Whistler Golf Club, designed by Arnold Palmer, is not overmatched by either the breathtaking scenery or the challenging skiing that takes place here in the winter.

It was this community's ultimately unhealthy dependence on solely winter activities that led it, in 1979, to begin the transformation into a year-round vacation playground. Whistler Golf Club was the first priority. While the theory was sound, achieving the reality proved to be a challenge, to say the least. Financial troubles aside, the proposed site in its glorious setting hid a myriad of design and construction nightmares. Much of the site was bog and had to be drained, underground springs had to be controlled and mountain runoff channelled. But three years of labor at about $1 million per year brought the course to fruition. Palmer should be commended for his compact design. Although it covers an economical 126 acres in this mountain-encircled bowl, there is never a sense of claustrophobia and the holes are admirably separated from both the safety and esthetic senses.

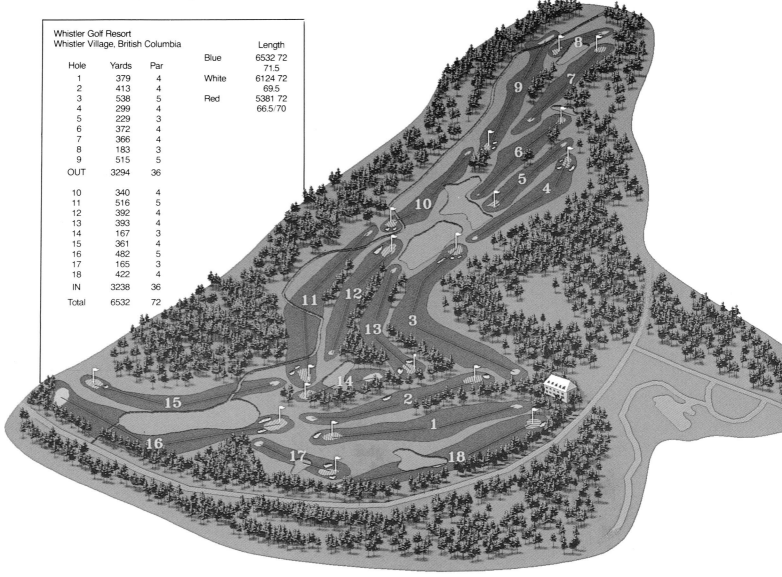

Whistler Golf Resort
Whistler Village, British Columbia

Hole	Yards	Par
1	379	4
2	413	4
3	538	5
4	299	4
5	229	3
6	372	4
7	366	4
8	183	3
9	515	5
OUT	3294	36
10	340	4
11	516	5
12	392	4
13	393	4
14	167	3
15	361	4
16	482	5
17	165	3
18	422	4
IN	3238	36
Total	6532	72

	Length	
Blue	6532	72
	71.5	
White	6124	72
	69.5	
Red	5381	72
	66.5/70	

A rocky-banked creek bisects the par-five 11th not once, but twice.

Players expecting climb up and down mountains all day are in for a surprise: management calls this "a mountain golf course you don't have to be a mountain goat to play." The entire course is relatively flat, but the snow-capped peaks of Whistler, Blackcomb and other mountains which encircle the layout remind you that this is indeed British Columbia. Where else, ask the locals, is it possible to ski and golf on the same day — without ever getting in a car?

Although Palmer was noted for his heroics on the golf course during his illustrious career (60 PGA Tour victories), the vacationers who play this 1983 creation would be better advised to avoid heroics. Mid- to high-handicap golfers will be able to enjoy their round simply by keeping the ball on the fairway and not trying to take advantage of the extra distance afforded by the thin mountain air or attempting to

duplicate Arnie's often miraculous shot-making. Trees, water and rough await those who bite off more than they can chew.

The first hole, a straightaway par-four, sets the tone for the round, gently urging the golfer to get away quickly — players are expected to play in under four hours, and marshalls are vigilant. Four hours is not unreasonable at most courses, especially one like Whistler that is not unreasonably long or tricky. But the first green sounds a note of caution as well. Not overly large, it nonetheless provides an adequate target. Once on, your putting line requires study. Should you be off the green, tangled rough and a horseshoe of trees will guarantee a bogey, or worse.

The Number 1 stroke hole is the third, a 538-yard par-five from the blue tees, 485 from the whites. This dogleg-right calls for a fade off the tee and, unless you are determined to

Crabapple Creek and nine ponds can make life miserable for the less-than-cautious player.

The Toughest Hole at Whistler Golf Club

The par-four 13th hole at Whistler Golf Club not only is a bear, it has — or had — a bear. Bear Island is a battleship-sized rock formation covered with spruce trees that shoots up out of the earth in the corner of this dramatic dogleg-left. Local legend has it that this rock formation got its nickname when a hapless golfer went into the woods to look for his ball and found a bear that wasn't named Jack Nicklaus. The hole plays into the prevailing wind and requires at least a 250-yard drive from the blue tees to give the player a legitimate shot at the large, very undulating and well-bunkered green. Bear Island prevents the big hitters from trying to cut the corner, while shorter hitters should veer to the extreme right to have any chance at the green. Assuming an ideal drive, the second shot will be slightly blind and could be anything from a three-iron to a wedge which will have to battle a fierce crosswind.

try to get home in two, a three-wood might be in order. A river describes the right boundary while deep woods await on the right.

For many golfers, the 11th hole poses the toughest test, because of the recurring presence of that most unforgiving of hazards: water. This 500-yard dogleg-left features Crabapple Creek not once, but twice. The meandering trout stream crosses the fairway from right-to-left at the corner of the dogleg and then makes another unwelcome appearance when it cuts

back again in front of the green. The creek comes into play as well on the ninth, 10th, 12th, 15th and 16th holes, and nine lakes of varying sizes claim their share of balls as well. But the creek didn't deter Palmer when he played an exhibition round to celebrate the opening of the course. In the fairway off the tee on Number 11, he lashed a two-wood to within five feet of the stick. Not recommended for beginners.

"Keep the ball down," Head Professional

Scott Staley advises first-time players at Whistler. In the heat of the summer, from mid-June until mid-August, powerful thermals sweep up the coast from Squamish to the south. "The wind starts at about 11 a.m. and by 1 p.m., there could be a three-club difference." The wind makes the most impact on holes nine through 13. "When the wind is up, I just try to get through that stretch at even-par," says Staley, who holds the course record of 65. "If I do that, I should have a solid round."

He also cautions that approach shots should be carefully considered. "These are typical Palmer greens and three putts are not unusual. There are a good number of bunkers and they are extremely well-placed. In general, they punish a short approach on the right. You've got to have a good short game to score well here."

In testimony to the foresight of the city fathers and the quality of Palmer's design, Whistler Golf Club is usually jammed. The arrival of courses by noted architects Robert Trent Jones and Jack Nicklaus soon may alleviate this pressure when they are fully on stream. In any case, this trio will certainly make Whistler Village, complete with its convention centre and wide range of accommodations and activities, the premier golf destination in Canada.

You must keep the ball down at Whistler, whether on approach shots or on par-threes such as No. 8.

Of the 27 holes at St. Charles, the South Course is noted for an abundance of trees.

ST. CHARLES

Country Club

Architects: Alister Mackenzie and Donald Ross
Head Professional: Jim Collins
Manager: Donald Cutler
Superintendent: Curtis Collins

"When you speak of a country club, you may feel inclined to merely associate it with that set which lingers on the clubhouse verandah at a Saturday-night dance, or simply killing time because there is nothing else to do. This is not true of St. Charles where top-level direction, sound planning and a great love for the contest, has left it as a monument to those founders who believed there should be a place where a fellow could enjoy good golf . . .plus several other sports in their day . . .where he and his family and their associates could enjoy a pleasant, social atmosphere in the best of the private-club practices."

So reads, in part, the preface to the club history of the St. Charles Country Club, established in 1905 and still maintaining those tenets which make it a model club. As vital to this reputation as the 27 holes designed by two of the world's best architects is the continuity and quality of the club's staff. At present, notes the club newsletter, "the club is in a very healthy financial position, our membership is full with a waiting list, and our club continues to be a very active club where our facilities are well supported and enjoyed by the majority of the members."

St. Charles Country Club Winnipeg, Manitoba				North Nine Hole	Yards	Par	West Nine		
				1	382	4	1	526	5
North-West	Length	Par	Rating	2	401	4	2	362	4
Blue	6466	72	71	3	268	4	3	373	4
White	6213	72	70	4	398	4	4	223	3
Yellow	5775	72	72	5	481	5	5	478	5
				6	130	3	6	359	4
West/South				7	378	4	7	194	3
Blue	6512	72	71	8	200	3	8	373	4
White	6234	72	70	9	560	5	9	380	4
Yellow	5780	72	72	Total	3198	36	Total	3268	36
South/ North				South Nine					
Blue	6442	72	71	1	342	4			
White	6219	72	71	2	158	3			
Yellow	5901	72	71	3	409	4			
				4	509	5			
				5	530	5			
				6	167	3			
				7	357	4			
				8	342	4			
				9	430	4			
				Total	3244	36			

Such was the intent of the founders in 1905 when they set the tone for what has come to be the province's most prominent golf club by entertaining the governor-general of Canada that year in the first major function of the St. Charles Country Club. The club grounds were also the site of the first polo matches in Manitoba, a pastime that occupied many members until the 1930s. Although the polo grounds have since been transformed into part of the golf course, one corner of the locker room continues to be known as the Polo Room. Croquet, steeplechasing, tennis and trapshooting were other popular ways to pass the time in the early days of St. Charles.

As with many private clubs, St. Charles came into being as a result of the efforts of a group of businessmen. In this case, 23 community leaders met in a bank in 1904 and decided to purchase 200 acres about 12 kilometres west of Winnipeg for $20,000. A clubhouse, stable, water tank and windmill were budgeted for at a cost of $50,000. A Mr. Pearson received the princely sum of $100 to design nine holes. To cover the expenditures, debentures would be sold for $100 with an entrance fee of $50. Dues would be $25 for gentlemen, $10 for ladies. Because of the relative isolation of the

The bunkers at St. Charles do not have overhanging lips or other punitive features, offering relatively easy outs to even high-handicappers.

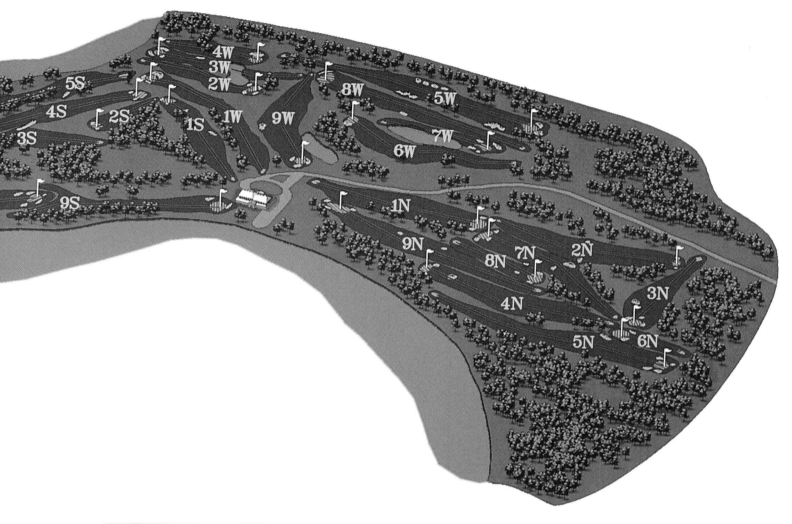

The Kid from St. Charles

The Kid started at St. Charles in 1947 at the age of 10, shagging balls on the range. At that time no one realized he would become one of the best ball-strikers in the history of the game. George Knudson won more PGA Tour tournaments, eight in all, than any other Canadian, despite not having a complete game. "His swing was very close to (Ben) Hogan's and a lot of people thought he was going to be the next Hogan," said Lee Trevino. "Unfortunately, he also had Hogan's putting stroke." Jack Nicklaus characterized him as "a million-dollar player, but a 10-cent putter." Nonetheless, he managed to win the Phoenix and Tucson Opens back-to-back in 1968. He nearly won consecutive tournaments again in 1972 when he won the Kaiser International and the following week led the Sahara Invitational by three strokes with one round left. He finished with a 76 and tied for seventh. He won two Canadian PGA Championships, the Ontario Open, was individual titleist in the 1966 World Cup and won several times on the Caribbean Tour. At the 1969 Masters, he finished second to George Archer. Ever the perfectionist, he said he had hit only one perfect golf shot in his entire life: a five-iron in Japan. After retiring from competitive golf, Knudson deeply influenced Canadian golf, devoting himself to teaching, writing an instruction book and developing a comprehensive teaching manual for the Canadian Professional Golfers' Association. He died in 1989 from cancer as he was about to embark on the Senior PGA Tour.

The well-groomed St. Charles layout is the consummate members' course.

club, a road had to be built and paid for by the membership at a cost of $300 a mile. A club rule specified a speed limit of 15 miles an hour and offenders were fined by the club.

St. Charles had the wisdom to employ two of the world's finest course designers, Alister Mackenzie and Donald Ross. In fact, Mackenzie and Ross were selected the best course architects in history in a GOLF magazine survey in 1988. Ross, responsible for the incomparable Pinehurst courses in South Carolina, designed the West Nine at St. Charles. A prolific architect, his designs are noted for their naturalness and links-like mounding inherited from his birthplace in Dornoch, Scotland.

Ross returned in 1920 to redesign the original nine and build what now is known as the West Nine. Those holes have undergone a number of changes under the direction of Canadian architects. Stanley Thompson renovated all the greens in 1947 and, in 1956, Norman Woods redesigned the entire layout. At present, Bill Robinson is responsible for

design improvements on the 27 holes which are played in different combinations every day to provide the members and their guests with an ever-changing challenge.

As for Mackenzie's influence on the North Nine, distinguished architect Robert Trent Jones says, "There was a dramatic boldness about his work; his bunkers were massive sprawls of sand, many with towering faces which, viewed from a distance, gave a concave appearance to the interior slopes, and his greens were extremely strongly contoured and many were hemmed with mounds. . . .His greens had a free-flowing sweep and grandeur to them." Although Mackenzie is responsible for courses on four continents, he is best remembered for Augusta National, permanent site of The Masters tournament.

While St. Charles is pre-eminently a members' club, those members have opened their course to some of the finest golfers in Canada and the world at various times. Regional, provincial, national and international championships have all been held here. The 1936 and 1957 Canadian Amateurs were at St. Charles, as were the Canadian Ladies' Open and Close in other years. The 1952 Canadian Open here is best remembered for the stellar performance of Johnny Palmer of North Carolina, who shot a record-breaking 66-65-66-66 — 263, 25 under par! In 1965, the course was the site of the Americas Cup, a team competition between Canada, the United States and Mexico. The winning Canadian team involved some of this country's all-time greats: Nick Weslock, Gary Cowan, Bill Pidlaski, Doug Silverberg, Keith Alexander, Johnny Johnston and Bert Ticehurst. Hall-of-Famer Bruce

Forbes was the non-playing captain.

Jim Collins, head professional at St. Charles since 1961, says all three nines are about equal in challenge, and play is rotated daily so members get a regular taste of each. "The South has lots of trees, the West has water in play on six holes and the North, while it has no water, is much narrower than the other nines.

"This course may not be a tremendous challenge for a very low handicapper," he acknowledges. "It is a good members' course; it's hard to lose golf balls, because it's so well groomed, and it's got a grandiose clubhouse with lots of room. Our members really enjoy it." Just the way they planned it, back in 1905.

The intriguing par-three seventh hole on the West Course, where water comes into play on six of the nine holes.

Mactaquac sprawls over more than 7,000 yards of New Brunswick countryside and features huge bunkers and greens.

— Mouth of Keswick, New Brunswick —

MACTAQUAC

Provincial Park Golf Course

Architect: William Mitchell
Head Professional: Alan Howie
Superintendent: Ken Creighton
Manager: Gary Albert

Mactaquac's designer, William Mitchell, has been credited with coining the term "executive course" for short golf courses made up of only par-threes and short par-fours. After he created Mactaquac for the New Brunswick government, almost every other course must have seemed that short by comparison. Opened in 1970, this expansive layout in a park not far from the provincial capital of Fredericton can play longer than 7,000 yards, and big hitters can really let out the shaft here.

"Mactaquac is one of the great courses in the East," says Stephen Ross, executive-director of the Royal Canadian Golf Association. His responsibilities have included selecting and setting up courses from coast to coast for national championships. "This course is built for championship conditions. The greens are big and can be made very fast. The terrain is excellent and the bentgrass fairways are great. The design allows for a variety of tee positions and the bunkers at Mactaquac are superb. It's a public course that rivals the best private clubs."

Between 25,000 and 30,000 rounds are played on the farflung environs of Mactaquac from May 1 until October 15 every year. "Every hole is so separate from all the others that you hardly ever

see anyone else," says Head Professional Alan Howie. "We have a lot of land here and that, combined with the many trees, means you're really insulated from the other holes. There are very few parallel holes and you hardly every hear 'Fore!'" A major concern at a public course of this calibre and potential difficulty is slow play but Howie says management has taken care of that by hiring a retired military officer to act as the course ranger. "He takes the job seriously and really speeds things up. It takes about 4 1/2 hours to play this course."

Mactaquac sprawls over beautifully rolling New Brunswick countryside, and "big" is a description that is appropriate for everything from the greens, tees and bunkers to the name of the golf course itself. While booster rockets may be required off the tee on some of the par-fives, those enormous greens call for careful study of the day's pin position. The greens have been likened to "parking lots at the end of each hole" and being short and having the

Mactaquac Provincial Park Golf Course
Mouth of Keswick, New Brunswick

	Length	Par	Rating
Blue	7,002	72	74
White	6,401	72	71
Gold	5,746	72	71

Hole	Yards	Par
1	480	5
2	384	4
3	402	4
4	146	3
5	343	4
6	384	4
7	476	5
8	192	3
9	393	4
OUT	3200	36

Hole	Yards	Par
10	384	4
11	384	4
12	453	5
13	183	3
14	375	4
15	480	5
16	178	3
17	394	4
18	393	4
IN	3224	36
Total	6424	72

option to chip it close may be preferable to an extremely long putt. In fairness, Mitchell restrained himself when contouring the putting surfaces, so most putts are straightforward. Be aware when selecting clubs that distances on the scorecard appear in metres, not yards. One metre equals 1.09 yards.

If you are going to gain a couple of shots on par at the 'Quac, try to make your move on holes four through seven, says Howie. "You could call this the birdie stretch. Number 4 is a short par-three with no trouble and a simple green. The fifth hole, I think, is the easiest par-four on the course. It's short, about 350 yards, with trees on the right but no trouble left. It's just a drive and a flip wedge, really, although the green is well-bunkered. The sixth is another relatively short par-four of about 370 yards. It's straightaway with trees on the right and left. A good drive is important and then you're left with a short-iron in. There's only one greenside bunker and that's on the left. The seventh hole is a reachable par-five about 480 yards in length. It's straight and wide-open although there are two fairway bunkers — one out about 200 yards that you

can carry on the drive and another short of the green. This green is elevated and can be tough to hold. There are two bunkers at the green, one in front and one left."

Howie has served at some of the finest private clubs in Canada, including Royal Ottawa Golf Club and Point Grey Golf and Country Club in Vancouver, but he swears he is being objective when he states that Mactaquac "is every bit as good as the best private clubs." Not only is the course well-maintained, complete with the decorative touches such as dainty flowerbeds seen at the posh private courses, but Howie says it has advantages over almost every other layout in Canada. "The length, the excellent bunkering and the great greens have convinced me that this is one of the very few courses in Canada that is capable of hosting a PGA Tour event," says the proud pro. "At the top of the list, of course, are the National, Glen Abbey and Royal Montreal. But we've got so much room, we could stretch the course to well over 7,000 yards and we have lots of space for galleries."

Mactaquac has played host to some of the finest players in the nation, including the cream

The well-bunkered 8th green requires a precise approach shot.

of Canada's amateurs in the 1986 championship. Brent Franklin of Calgary shot a course-record 67 under perfect conditions on his way to his second consecutive Canadian Amateur title. He won again the next year. Only Franklin and Jack Kay Jr. of Toronto managed to keep their four-round scores under par.

"It's a very good golf course," says Douglas Brewer, chairman of the course's advisory board since 1969. "The premier at the time, Louis Robichaud, had it in his mind to build a public golf course that could host national championships and that's been accomplished. Robichaud had taken up the game three or four years previously and was very keen. He liked to get personally involved in the project.

"Certainly, the Parks people worked very hard in the early years to make Mactaquac a showpiece, although I am concerned about the future budget situation," says Brewer, a past-president of the Royal Canadian Golf Association.

The expansive, well-treed layout means other groups are seldom seen.

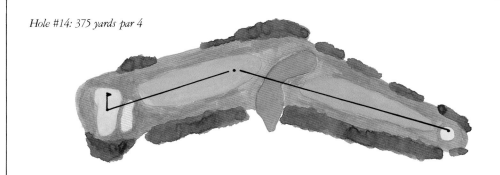

Hole #14: 375 yards par 4

Very few public courses offer the facilities, conditioning and challenge found at Mactaquac.

The Toughest Hole at Mactaquac

"The 14th hole here can make or break your round," says Alan Howie, head professional at Mactaquac Provincial Park Golf Course. This 375-yard par-four features a pond running across the fairway in an awkward spot. "You can either hit a seven-iron off the tee and then a two- or a three-iron in, or try to carry the ball about 220 yards over the water and have a seven- or eight-iron in. There are woods left and right as well as a big bunker in front of a relatively flat green. Watch out if the pin position is back left; that's the most difficult because you have to hit over that huge bunker."

Renovations to the Donald Ross-designed Riverside Country Club have rejuvenated the many bunkers, like these on the par-four first hole.

RIVERSIDE

Country Club

Architect: Donald Ross
Head Professional: Jim Connolly
Superintendent: Brian Gouthro

The roots of the Riverside Country Club, one of the most prestigious golf clubs in Atlantic Canada, go back almost 100 years to when a group of prominent citizens of Saint John decided to purchase land for a course. Things appeared auspicious right from the start. Keeping in mind that it is often difficult when perusing the histories of golf clubs to separate fact from fiction, the story is told that the first shot of the first game ever played on this rudimentary layout (then called the Saint John Golf Club) in 1896 was a hole-in-one!

Although the club moved in 1912 from that locale to a splendid site overlooking the brawny Kennebecasis River, visitors still sense the tradition and pride that characterize Riverside. Its rich tournament record includes the 1939 Canadian Open, the first ever played outside Ontario or Quebec and won by Harold (Jug) McSpaden, several Canadian Amateurs and numerous other national championships. Its emphasis on continuity is obvious from the moment you enter the pro shop. Head Professional Jim Connolly has been here since 1959, having started as a 12-year-old caddie.

Connolly has seen considerable remodelling from the original Donald Ross design in his four decades. Architect Bill Robinson

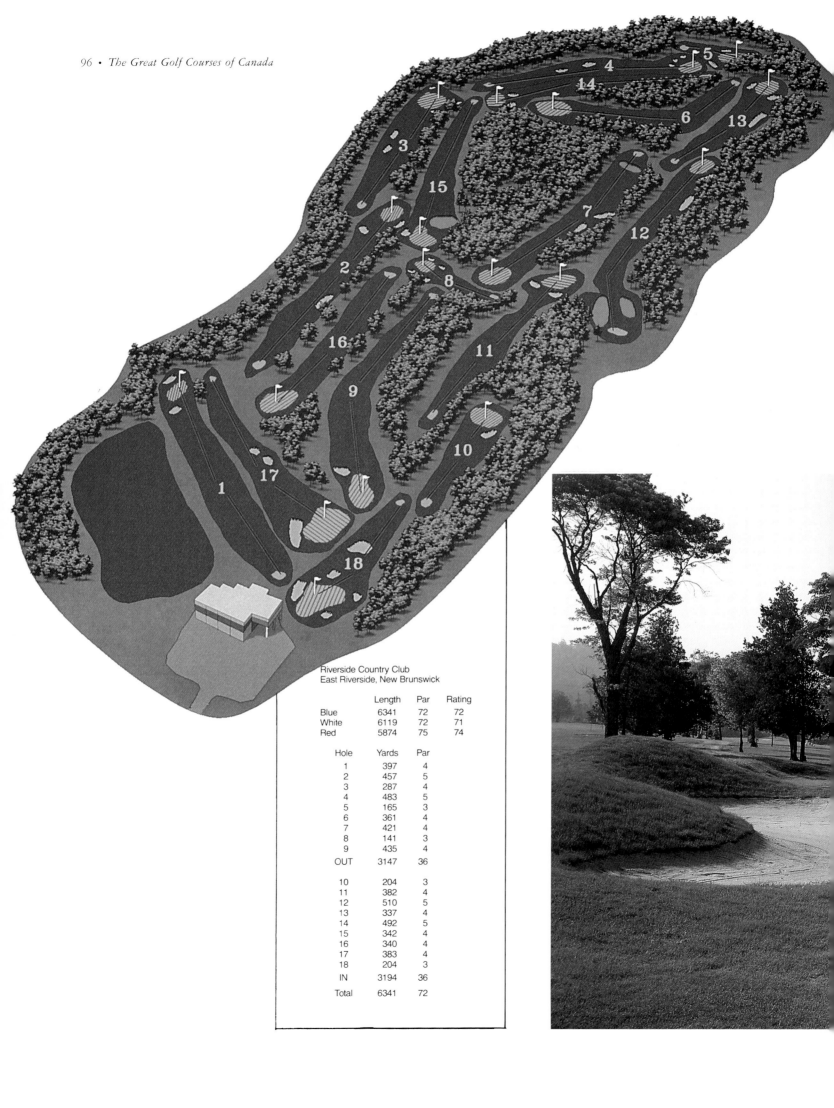

Riverside Country Club
East Riverside, New Brunswick

	Length	Par	Rating
Blue	6341	72	72
White	6119	72	71
Red	5874	75	74

Hole	Yards	Par
1	397	4
2	457	5
3	287	4
4	483	5
5	165	3
6	361	4
7	421	4
8	141	3
9	435	4
OUT	3147	36
10	204	3
11	382	4
12	510	5
13	337	4
14	492	5
15	342	4
16	340	4
17	383	4
18	204	3
IN	3194	36
Total	6341	72

of White Rock, B.C., has been laboring on Riverside since 1988. "Bill has restructured every trap on the golf course," Connolly noted. "Golf courses are like people; they get old. We're continually trying to keep it revitalized for our membership."

A round at Riverside is a reminder that while it's all well and good to be able to hit a long ball, the shots around and on the greens are critical for good scoring. When playing with a member, pick his brain for tips on each green. Although many putts may appear straight, be assured that there are significant unseen breaks on all 18 putting surfaces. A two-putt is a triumph in many cases.

The opening hole, a 385-yard par-four, offers a generous landing area. A short-iron approach may require one more club because the green is slightly elevated. The second and third holes present birdie chances, although danger awaits on both. Number 2 is a 450-yard par-five. Aim for the right fairway bunker in order to have the best chance of reaching the green in two. Stay away from the bush on the left at all costs. Like most wooded holes at Riverside, a ball hit into the bush is most likely a ball lost. Do not be deceived by what the scorecard says about the third hole. A seemingly frail 285-yard par-four, this hole plays straight uphill. Following a good drive, a less-than-accurate wedge can turn your birdie hopes into a three-putt bogey.

Riverside's fourth is rated the most difficult hole on the course. Again, the uninitiated may glance at the card and see a 472-yard par-five and consider it another opportunity to gain a stroke on par. But this tight dogleg-right causes more sixes than fours to be written on scorecards. The lumpy fairway falls off left into tangled rough while the entire right side is defined by a continuous stand of mature hardwoods and evergreens. Assuming a well-placed drive, gambling for the green in two may not be worth the risk. The ever-narrowing fairway

Traps and mounds surrounded the 11th green at Riverside.

funnels into a miniscule, well-trapped green, and accuracy on the approach is essential.

Riverside is notable as well for its fine par-threes and the fifth hole is a classic. At 160 yards, you have no option but to hit a mid-iron to the green because there is no bail-out area; mounds, traps and rough encircle the putting surface.

After a brief respite provided by the 356-yard sixth hole, you start to negotiate what is known as the toughest stretch on the course: holes seven through 11. While none overwhelms with length, all place unrelenting demands on your shotmaking ability.

The ideal drive on the seventh, a 413-yard par-four rated as the most difficult hole on the course, will be left-centre. When hitting the mid-iron approach shot, make sure you

have enough club to get to the green; a slight rise in front prevents a short attempt from rolling on. Number 8 calls for, appropriately enough, an eight-iron for most players. Its well-trapped green also provides for some tough pin placements. And if you think you've seen difficult greens thus far, wait for Number 9, a 431-yard par-four. "A treacherous green," says Connolly, "even more so than the others. And be careful on your tee shot, because everything rolls to the river." A laser-like long-iron must be struck through a narrow opening on the par-three 10th to a green surrounded by trees and boasting a pot bunker in front. Riverside's "lethal linkage" of five testing holes finishes with the 341-yard 11th which calls for a mid-iron to a narrow, well-trapped green.

An unusual aspect of Riverside is the fin-

Eagles Beat Birdies

The 1975 Canadian Amateur at Riverside Country Club provided a rare level of golf excitement. Ralph Costello, in his book "The First Fifty Years," relates how Jim Nelford of Burnaby, B.C., and Gary Cowan of Kitchener, Ontario, battled for the title. After 63 holes, the two were tied. Cowan, a dominating force with two U.S. Amateur victories under his belt, responded to the challenge with back-to-back birdies — and still lost two strokes to Nelford. Costello remembers how Nelford's five-iron approach on the par-five 14th stopped 15 feet away from the pin. Cowan also was on in two shots but needed two putts to Nelford's one. On the next hole, a downhill par-four to a tiny green guarded by a pond and bunkers, Nelford pushed his drive into trees to the right of the fairway. His second shot, which he hoped would reach the green at best, landed short, rolled onto the green and into the hole. Cowan's birdie was not enough to keep pace with Nelford's brilliance. Cowan, who eventually finished third behind Doug Roxburgh of Vancouver, summed it up by saying: "When you go birdie-birdie and lose two strokes, you know you're in trouble."

ishing hole: a 198-yard par-three. This testing hole plays downhill into the river valley and is marked by bunkers which bisect the fairway some 90 yards short of the green. Club selection is difficult, as is concentrating on the task at hand. The breathtaking beauty of the Kennebecasis River and the hills beyond only serve as delightful distractions which must be ignored until your tee shot is struck.

A cold Moosehead ale is called for in the comfortable, rambling clubhouse built in 1966. The former clubhouse burned down just as the present one was being completed. It seems some caddies were playing cards in the basement of the old clubhouse just prior to flames breaking out . . .fact or fiction?

An unusual touch: Riverside's finishing hole is a 200-yard par-three that demands length and accuracy.

The original Ashburn course in Halifax is the shorter but very challenging older brother of New Ashburn, the championship layout north of the city.

— Windsor Junction, Nova Scotia —

ASHBURN

Golf Club

Architects: Geoffrey Cornish & Bill Robinson
Head Professional: Kelly Burnett
Professional: John Scott
Manager: Douglas Connors

Perhaps the Ashburn Golf Club should more appropriately be called the Ashburn Golf Clubs. For there are indeed two very dissimilar Ashburn courses separated by some 30 kilometres. That's an important fact to remember, particularly if you arrive at Halifax airport and ask the taxi driver to take you to the "Ashburn Golf Club."

On one hand, the driver might take you to the original Ashburn Golf Club, which is closing in on its centennial year, having its roots back in 1896. To confuse the issue further, there's also a Halifax Golf and Country Club, which operates the Ashburn courses. The old course, a compact design by Stanley Thompson, is located in Armdale, near the heart of Halifax. Extensive renovation by Quebec architect Graham Cooke has ensured this venerable course remains a pleasant, yet challenging, facility for city players, especially juniors, seniors and women.

But lurking in the heavy woods outside Halifax, overlooking placid Kinsac Lake, is the sinister aspect of Ashburn's Jekyll-and-Hyde personality — a 7,000-yard spectre called New Ashburn, which was opened in 1970. This Cornish & Robinson design is a spectacularly strong layout, featuring fiendishly tilted fairways,

unyielding rough and large, fast greens. This combination of length, uneven lies and potential three-putt greens precludes many birdie chances. But that doesn't seem to matter to many of Ashburn's 1,100 members, the majority of whom travel to the more isolated new course to test their abilities.

And tested they will be, says noted amateur Graham MacIntyre. "There are two key stretches at New Ashburn: holes seven through 12 and 15 through 18." This is not to say that the others are weak sisters; they simply help build the suspense.

The seventh hole calls for a fade off the tee if the ball is to stay on the sloping fairway.

From the white tees, the accuracy of a two-iron may be in order on the 398-yard par-four. In any case, the premium is on a precise tee shot if you are to have any chance to par this exceptionally tough hole. A large hump in the green demands that you stay below the hole.

Any par-three that exceeds 230 yards is difficult by definition, but when you are hitting into a green that is traversed by several ridges and is as quick as the putting surfaces at New Ashburn, the difficulty factor goes off the scale. The trick on the eighth hole, advises MacIntyre, is to have enough club, particularly if the pin is at the back. Of course, if you can't hit the

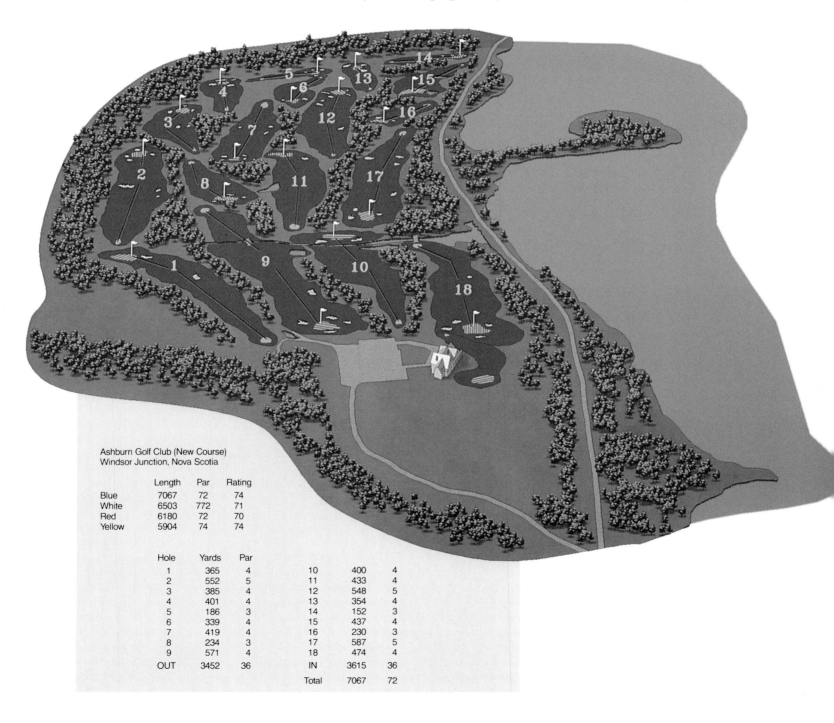

Ashburn Golf Club (New Course)
Windsor Junction, Nova Scotia

	Length	Par	Rating
Blue	7067	72	74
White	6503	772	71
Red	6180	72	70
Yellow	5904	74	74

Hole	Yards	Par			
1	365	4	10	400	4
2	552	5	11	433	4
3	385	4	12	548	5
4	401	4	13	354	4
5	186	3	14	152	3
6	339	4	15	437	4
7	419	4	16	230	3
8	234	3	17	587	5
9	571	4	18	474	4
OUT	3452	36	IN	3615	36
			Total	7067	72

ball 230 yards with any club in your bag, you have a problem.

Usually, the strategy on the 10th hole is to hit your tee shot as far down the hill as you can to avoid a sloping lie for your second shot. But if you are a big hitter playing from forward tees, be wary of the ponds that pinch either side of the fairway close to the green; you may want to leave the driver alone. This 378-yarder is a fine, pretty hole with a very quick green guarded by a creek and two bunkers. The 11th, says MacIntyre, is the toughest on the course. A par-four of well over 400 yards, the fairway is flanked by ponds and is well protected with huge cloverleaf-shaped bunkers. The green is difficult to read and very fast, especially back-to-front and on the left side.

Finishing this stretch is the fateful 12th, a long par-five which may induce you to relax with its relatively easy opening shot. After that, the real work begins. On the second shot, the rapidly narrowing fairway falls sharply right and is framed by bunkers. The severely sloped green, encircled by four traps, has claimed many victims, most frequently when the pin is back left. Chief among them may be present PGA Tour pro Richard Zokol of Vancouver who four-putted the 12th green. He was tied for the lead in the 1980 Canadian Amateur at the time.

Now is the time for one of those sighs of relief: the 13th and 14th holes are relatively docile birdie opportunities — if your nerves haven't been shattered to this point.

Stepping onto the 15th tee, don't allow the scenic beauty of this lengthy par-four to distract you from the task ahead. The drive calls for a slight draw around a tall tree positioned beside a pond in the fairway. If you have been reconnoitering this hole as you walked by on adjacent holes, you will realize that the second shot is fraught with problems. A spring-fed pond, unseen from the landing area, abuts the left side of the slightly elevated green while a bunker will devour shots hit to the right. In a rare example of generosity, the green is

Sloping fairways, narrow landing areas, hidden ponds and swales are typical of New Ashburn.

flat and comparatively simple to read.

The 16th hole may look familiar; another par-three of more than 200 yards with a severe, well-bunkered green. Accept a par here gratefully and move on to Number 17, a great par-five, especially from the blue tees. At 587 yards, 100 yards more than from the white blocks, the 17th is a very demanding hole. Its landing area is defined by three fairway bunkers and the second and third shots must be delicately placed.

In the 1980 Canadian Amateur, the par-four 18th hole was never played from the blue tees. At 474 yards, it was judged too long and difficult even for the top amateur players in the country. Par is never a certainty, even from the white tees which present a challenge by being tucked into the right side of the hole. The opening drive must be faded to keep it on the fairway, but stay away from the tree in left-centre. The three-level green is very slick from front-to-back and right-to-left, and must be treated with great respect.

Harking back again to the 1980 amateur championship, only one player, Stu Hamilton of Toronto, managed to register a sub-par round during the tournament, a one-under 70. The competitors in that event learned what New Ashburn's members had known for years: this course is a relentless, unforgiving layout that rewards only the finest efforts, and punishes all others mercilessly.

The old course is no pushover, either. The late George Knudson, an acknowledged master of the game, could manage no better than four under par on his way to winning the 1964 Canadian PGA Championship there. Forty years earlier, the caddies threatened to go on strike for more money because "20 cents per round is insufficient for so difficult a course."

The danger wasn't all on the course in those days. An entry in the club manager's diary from 1924 reveals that "Bandits shot Stephen Kennedy outside gates yesterday a.m." The manager, who no doubt was suitably shocked, reacted as any hard-core golfer would. "Went for round of golf in afternoon," the entry continues.

The "old" Ashburn course overlooks the harbor city of Halifax; the new course is cut from virgin forest on Kinsac Lake.

The 15th hole is well-trapped and includes a hidden water hazard for good measure.

Hole #9: 571 yards par 5

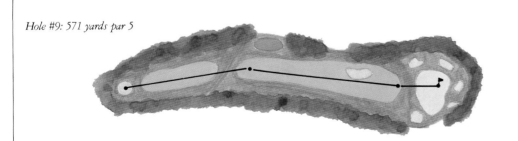

The Number 1 stroke hole at New Ashburn is the par-five ninth, 541 yards from the white tees, and 571 from the blues. It is a straightforward challenge with a tee shot over a brook that is not really in play. The pond on the left of the fairway is most definitely in play, however, and the landing area is relatively flat. From the landing area to the green is uphill, precluding getting home in two. Hitting three shots — driver, fairway wood and anything from a seven-iron to a wedge — is a realistic expectation. If you have your wits about you, you'll check out the pin position on Number 9 as you walk down the first fairway. Keep in mind that four-time national amateur champion Doug Roxburgh took a diastrous eight on this hole during the 1980 Canadian Amateur.

Known locally as "Killer," the long and narrow seventh hole is the toughest test at Highlands Links on Cape Breton Island.

———— *Ingonish Beach, Nova Scotia* ————

HIGHLANDS LINKS

Cape Breton Highlands National Park

Architect: Stanley Thompson
Head Professional: Joe Robinson
Superintendent: Martin Walsh

"This is the Cypress Point of Canada for sheer beauty," the late George Knudson once labelled Highlands Links. "When you're driving up the road to the course, it's like driving up to heaven."

Emerging from the fog which often enshrouds the top of Smoky Mountain, the highest point in Nova Scotia near the outermost tip of Cape Breton Island, awaits a heavenly golf experience indeed. For there, carved out of virgin forest 50 years ago, rests a rugged giant called Highlands Links.

When Stanley Thompson trekked to the wilds of Cape Breton at the invitation of the federal government, to build a course within the confines of Cape Breton Highlands National Park, he discovered a challenge appropriate for the man who constructed such wilderness gems as Banff Springs and Jasper Park.

"Stanley Thompson in his early days sometimes would use little more than instinct in laying out his courses . . . striving to retain as much of the natural ground formation as possible. The most beautiful courses, he is convinced — the ones where the greens invite your shots — are the ones which hew most closely to nature," John La Cerda wrote in the Saturday Evening Post in 1946. Highlands Links, like his glorious Capilano on Canada's western coast in West Vancouver, demonstrates the genius of Thompson's instinct.

Highlands Links Ingonish Beach, Nova Scotia				Hole	Yards	Par	Hole	Yards	Par
				1	413	4	10	151	3
				2	441	4	11	534	5
	Length	Par	Rating	3	143	3	12	227	3
Blue	6588	72	72	4	326	4	13	423	4
White	6193	71	71	5	164	3	14	411	4
Yellow	5659	76	73	6	532	5	15	548	5
				7	570	5	16	460	5
				8	314	4	17	190	3
				9	337	4	18	409	4
				OUT	3240	36	IN	3348	36
							Total	6588	72

Here, in the shadow of Mount Franey, within sight of the Atlantic Ocean and the Clyburn River, using manual labor and horsedrawn implements, Thompson created a masterpiece. It does not overpower with length (the course plays less than 6,600 yards from the tips), but rather with relentless demands on the golfer to produce the exact shot required.

Although the actual golf holes are not lengthy by modern standards, be prepared for a vigorous outing. The links-style course (nine holes out from the clubhouse and nine back) loops around an 11-kilometre routing. A walk from one green to the next tee may cover 300 metres or more, but the flora, fauna and

Like all the par-threes at Highlands Links, the 10th hole is pretty, but tough.

spectacular scenery make the exertion worthwhile. Golf carts are not available. "Take a box lunch out there, go out for 18 holes and you're gone for the day," Knudson advised.

On most holes, a level lie is the only reward for a perfectly placed shot; on some, the teeing ground offers the only flat surface. During construction, huge boulders were tumbled onto the fairways, covered with topsoil and seed, and have become massive moguls to be negotiated with extreme care. The greens, as inviting as Thompson may have intended them, are characterized by swales running through the surface and flanked by sand traps.

After negotiating the first hole, a 408-yard

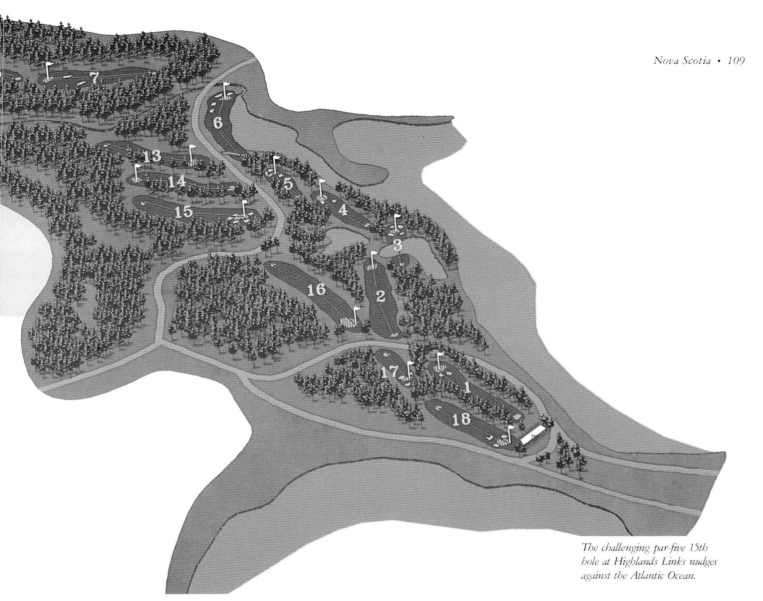

The challenging par-five 15th hole at Highlands Links nudges against the Atlantic Ocean.

par-four, you look back at the modest club-house, and beyond in stark contrast to the deep green forest covering Mount Franey, sits Keltic Lodge. With its white clapboard and red tile roof, the quaint, comfortable lodge (world-renowned for its lobster dinners) is only a few hundred metres from the course.

All the holes bear Gaelic names, as befits a course called Highlands Links. Some are humorous ("Muckle Mouth Meg"), others puzzling ("Tattie Bogle" translates as "potato pits"), but few are as appropriate as that affixed to the fourth hole: Heich O'Fash (Heap of Trouble).

Rated as the Number 1 stroke hole, the 270-yard 4th (Heich O' Fash) deceives the unwary or the over-confident player with its lack of length. An accurate tee shot will attain the top of a plateau which rises from the fairway about 150 yards out. Approach shots to the green, situated on a second plateau, must take into account the ugly fact that inaccuracy will be punished severely. Being left or right could mean a lost ball, while the cunningly sloped green may reject a less-than-perfect attempt and spit it into the trees and tangled

rough which surround the putting surface.

One of Thompson's trademarks, fairway bunkers some 30 yards short of the green, provide another unwelcome surprise on the fourth hole. First-time players may assume these bunkers are green-side and find themselves two or three clubs short on their approach. After surviving Heich O'Fash, glance right to see another emblem of Highlands Links' uniqueness: lobster dories tied up where the river juts into the adjacent fairway.

The seventh hole is called Killiecrankie, which translates as "a long and narrow pass," but perhaps the local nickname, "Killer," reveals more about its character. A 556-yard par-five, the seventh is rated the toughest hole on the course. Bounded by majestic maples, the narrow double-dogleg defends itself admirably from those long hitters who try to reach the green in two. Its defences include Highlands Links' ever-present uneven lies, and a huge bunker guarding the right side of the green. Your task is far from complete once on the

putting surface: a long, two-tiered green offers a myriad of pin locations.

On Number 15 (Tattie Bogle), the ideal tee shot requires a powerful blow over the hill on the left. The third shot on this 546-yard par-five is to a green, surrounded by five bunkers, which sits almost at the front doorstep of St. Paul's Church. First-time visitors are sometimes seen wandering through the adjacent graveyard, pulling golf carts, trying to find the 16th tee.

You may want to take a cue from some of the locals, who dip their golf balls into the holy water at St. Paul's on the way to Number 16. Aptly named Sair Fecht (Hard Work), this relatively short par-five is merciless, but a fantastic golf hole nonetheless. The opening drive on this 458-yarder must carry a ravine or it's "three from the tee." Only a slightly better fate awaits those who hit it straight, for the fairway undulations resemble the surface of the neighboring Atlantic during a winter storm. Picture a herd of buried elephants

---

One of the many unusual aspects of Highlands Links is the Gaelic names given to each hole. Some relate to an aspect of the hole, others were selected simply because of their colorful Scottish flavor. Photograph is of hole number 15, Tattie Bogle.

1. BEN FRANEY: Playing through this fairway presents a full view of Ben Franey. "Ben" is Scottish for "mountain."
2. TAM O'SHANTER: A Scot's bonnet is known as a Tam O'Shanter; in this case, the shape of the green is the reason for the appelation.
3. LOCHAN: A small sheet of water, or miniature lake.
4. HEICH O'FASH: Heap of trouble.
5. CANNY SLAP: A small opening, or "slap", in a hedge or fence.
6. MUCKLE MOUTH MEG: Reportedly, Muckle Mouth Meg, a Scottish lass from Hawick, could swallow a whole "Bubbly Jock's Egg" (a turkey egg).
7. KILLERCRANKIE: A long, narrow pass
8. CABER'S TOSS: The follow-through after tossing the caber (a log used during Highland games) can be described as "up and over."
9. CORBIE'S NEST: A corbie is a crow, while "nest" is high ground.
10. CUDDY'S LUGS: Donkey's ears. A description of the green.
11. BONNIE BURN: A pleasant stream.
12. CLEUGH: Cleugh is a term used for placenames in the Cheviot hills of Scotland. It means a deep gully or ravine with precipitous sides.
13. LAIRD: A Scottish land owner.
14. HAUGH: A small hollow or valley.
15. TATTIE BOGLE: Potato pits. Potatoes are placed in pits and covered with thatch.
16. SAIR FECHT: Hard work.
17. DOWIE DEN: The Scottish border ballad "The Dowie Dens of Yarrow" relates to a massacre.
18. HAME NOO: Home now.

trooping down the fairway and you have a fairly accurate idea of the lie you face.

Parks Canada has been criticized for not contributing enough money to adequately maintain this national treasure, but that situation appears to be improving. Highlands Links hired its first professionally trained course superintendent in 1990, and improve-

ments are noticeable already. This is a golf experience that, regretably, few Canadians have savored. It is guaranteed not to disappoint.

Members of other distinguished golf clubs in Atlantic Canada call Highlands Links "the best course in the world." After delighting in the wild, ethereal beauty of this unique links layout, you may be inclined to agree.

The swales and humps on the 14th hole are typical of the Stanley Thompson layout.

—————— *Aurora, Ontario* ——————

BEACON HALL

Golf and Country Club

Architect: Bob Cupp with Thomas McBroom
Head Professional: Phil Hardy
Manager: Gary Carl
Superintendent: Bob Heron

Beacon Hall has been called "the most exclusive golf club in Canada," and it may well be in terms of number of members. A mere 230 purists belong to this classically understated refuge built on a magnificent site north of Toronto. Indeed, only a handful of golf clubs in North America have a smaller membership roster. Membership at Beacon Hall is not something one brags about, but it is something to be very proud of — the course was ranked fifth in the country by SCORE, the national golf magazine, in its first year of eligibilty in 1990.

From the back tees, Beacon Hall approaches 7,000 yards, "a course for players of supreme ability," says course architect Bob Cupp, himself a former PGA Tour pro. "Though they are few, they do have a tremendous influence over the reputation of the course." Cupp says that while the course could host any tournament from a stategic point of view, due to the underlying philosophy of the wealthy members to shun publicity, "there will be no accommodations for gallery or tournament operations. This is a course for the members — but with enough teeth to gain the respect of even the severest critics." This is not to say that Cupp's design excludes players of lesser ability: "The members' course will be

all of the members' course," he says, and it is true that the other tee postions offer a gratifying, yet challenging, test.

The very existence of Beacon Hall is gratifying as well to those few individuals who, concerned about crowded conditions at other Toronto private clubs, decided to assemble a group to purchase the former Toronto and North York Hunt Club and an adjacent farm to give Cupp the land he needed to create a "world-class" facility. As well, 80 attractive, expensive and unobtrusive housing units were planned: their sale would provide true aficionados with a residence on one of the country's finest course and assist with the project's financing. Cupp was impressed by the group's efforts, calling the 260 acres the best piece of property he had ever had the opportunity to work with. The result, which opened in 1988, is a golfer's dream: a masterful routing taking full advantage of the property's varying personalties. "Every shot will be presented like

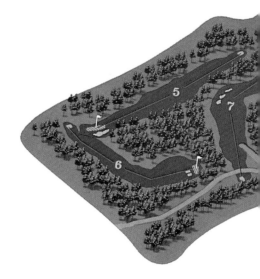

The third hole at Beacon Hall winds through pines reminiscent of the Carolinas.

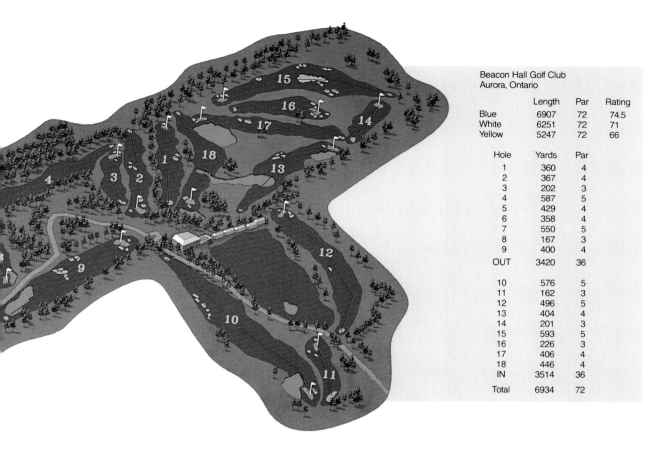

Beacon Hall Golf Club Aurora, Ontario			
	Length	Par	Rating
Blue	6907	72	74.5
White	6251	72	71
Yellow	5247	72	66
Hole	Yards	Par	
1	360	4	
2	367	4	
3	202	3	
4	587	5	
5	429	4	
6	358	4	
7	550	5	
8	167	3	
9	400	4	
OUT	3420	36	
10	576	5	
11	162	3	
12	496	5	
13	404	4	
14	201	3	
15	593	5	
16	226	3	
17	406	4	
18	446	4	
IN	3514	36	
Total	6934	72	

a picture," Cupp resolved when designing the course, and he delivered on that promise.

The first four holes play through towering red pines reminiscent of the Carolinas, and then the vegetation makes a pleasing switch to burly hardwoods — maples, oaks and walnuts. The back nine, with its mammoth sand hill and swales swathed in native grasses, takes the player on an imaginary and tactical visit to the links courses of Scotland and Ireland. The finishing hole unites the features in summary; looking back off the tee, adjacent to the first green and its protective pines, your eyes pan across the sandy mounds of the back nine, but your drive must carry uphill through more hardwoods.

"I think Bob Cupp designed the course beautifully," says Head Professional Phil Hardy. "The first six holes combine a gentle invitation to the course with a taste of what's to come. The next six say, 'Here's where you make your move,' with their three par-fives. The final six are all golf. They've killed a lot of hopes. I've seen great players come to 15, 16, 17 or 18 at- or under-par and walk off the course without finishing."

That last stretch obviously is key to a good round at Beacon Hall. It commences with Number 13, a 400-yard par-four with a generous fairway, inviting the player to "bust it," says Cupp. As on many of the holes, the fairway bunkers — on the left in this case — indicate the best postion. "At this course, the fairway bunkers are usually saying, 'Come as close to me as you dare,'" says Hardy. "They indicate where you have the best approach, where you will have the most green to work with." On 13, you are penalized if you don't flirt with these traps: an approach from anywhere else must carry over a particularly nasty greenside bunker.

The next hole plays 199 yards from the back tees. This claustrophic par-three is hemmed in on three sides by mounds or hills. The green is guarded by two bunkers, one of which is three metres deep. If you are playing the white tees, play safe to the left and bounce the ball onto the green, advises Cupp.

The par-five 15th hole presents a heroic challenge from the tee. Its split fairway is separated by a waste bunker the size of a football field — one acre in area. The short, or left, route requires precision to place the ball in a landing area only 30 yards wide, but offers

The first hole at Beacon Hall slopes away from the clubhouse, inviting the player into what is guaranteed to be a memorable round.

the successful gambler a long-iron approach to a severely contoured green guarded by three bunkers on the right. The player who elects to stay right and hope for par must follow Cupp's prescription: A drive to the corner of the dogleg, a long-iron or fairway wood near a bunker set in a mogul on the right side and then a wedge to cover the remaining 80 or 90 yards to the two-tiered green.

"If there is a supreme test at Beacon Hall, this is it," says Cupp about the par-three 16th, and everyone who has played the course agrees with him. At 228 yards from the blue tees and 213 from the whites, this hole may require more club than some players have in their bags, especially if played into the wind. The intervening area between the elevated tee and green is layered in tall, waving fescue grass

and swallows any errant shot, although there is a landing area left of the green.

The 17th hole, a straightaway par-four, reiterates one of the underlying design principles at Beacon Hall: play as close as you can to the fairway bunkers on the right because the green opens up fully from that side. Being in the left greenside bunker means playing out of the sand directly toward a pond — not a desireable scenario.

As mentioned, the finishing hole combines all the esthetic qualities of the property, but it also presents the final strategic challenge of the round. A good drive on this lengthy par-four (448 from the blues, 409 from the whites) will be followed by a long-iron toward the well-mounded and -bunkered green near the clubhouse.

Hole #4: 587 yards par 5

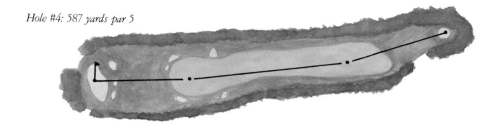

The Toughest Hole at Beacon Hall

The 587-yard fourth hole, the first par-five encountered at Beacon Hall, is rated the most difficult hole on the course. In the words of course designer Bob Cupp, "The drive will be played from an elevated tee across a depression to a fairway rising and winding to the right. The tee shot from the white and yellow markers will be substantially farther forward, but uphill. Once the players successfully reaches the first landing area, the next challenge is reaching the second landing area and 'setting up' the approach. The second landing area is actually in the shape of a giant green, nearly 47,000 square feet — about an acre — and a fair challenge for the three-wood or long-iron required to get there. From anywhere on the second landing area, the green will be visible and a fair target. The shot to the green will be the first true test of the round. The putting surface lies at the top of a rise. Three bunkers rest in the front slope of the green area. The back is supported by low mounds. Anything over the green will roll down the backslope; a formidable hazard."

The greens at Beacon Hall are straightforward; the challenge is to get to them in regulation.

Brantford is a splendid retreat set among mature maples and oaks. Here, the par-four eleventh hole.

BRANTFORD

Golf and Country Club

Architect: Thompson, Cumming and Thompson
Head Professional: Jeff Bentley
Manager: Iain MacLean
Superintendent: Vince Piccolo

In January 1879, the following notice appeared in The Courier, the newspaper serving the southwestern Ontario city of Brantford: "A golf club (whatever that may mean) has been organized in this city with the following as office bearers: A. Robertson, captain; John H. Stratford, treasurer; W.L. Creighton, secretary; Henry Yates, Jas. Ker Osborne, J.Y. Morton, George H. Wilkes, committee. They will play Wednesdays and Fridays." Later that year, these stalwarts were joined by Hon. A.S. Hardy, the premier of Ontario and the first cabinet minister in Canada to join a golf club, and Alfred J. Wilkes.

From its initial four-hole start atop the inauspiciously named Vinegar Hill, Brantford Golf and Country Club moved to other locales which featured the game of golf in its most rudimentary sense. It was not until the third course was established that any attempt was made to maintain decent greens and tees and install bunkers. Annual dues were $2 for men, $1 for ladies, and a caretaker was charged with cutting the greens and tees. The club history notes that "he was helped by a herd of cattle which grazed on the course."

Brantford Golf and Country Club joined the Toronto Golf Club,

The par-three third hole at Brantford plays 165 yards downhill.

which was founded in 1876 as the first golf club in North America west of Montreal, as the only courses in Ontario. They, bolstered by players from a new club at Niagara-on-the-Lake, soon challenged a Quebec provincial team, consisting of members from Royal Montreal (founded in 1873) and Royal Quebec (1874). These first interprovincial matches were held in Montreal in 1882 and, despite the stellar play of Brantford member A.W. Smith, Quebec dominated. Ontario would have its revenge the following year, defeating Quebec by 30 holes.

Two more moves were made before 1906 when nine holes were laid out in the vicinity of the present course. But a rapidly growing membership demanded an expansion of both the course and the clubhouse, necessitating the purchase of adjacent land in 1919. The course was designed by Thompson, Cumming and Thompson, a Toronto partnership of brothers Stanley and Nicol Thompson and George Cumming, the head professional at the Toronto Golf Club. While it would be Stanley who developed into the dean of Canada's course architects, the history of the Brantford Golf and Country Club ascribes most of the credit

for this design to Cumming and Nicol, who served as head professional at the Hamilton Golf and Country Club in Ancaster, Ontario, for 50 years.

The outstanding periodical of the time, Canadian Golfer, described their handiwork: "A very sporting course is this 18-hole course on the banks of the Grand River. The total length is 6,300 yards. There are three one-shot holes, three three-shot holes, whilst the balance are two-shot holes — the backbone of every well-designed course. There are many holes of surpassing merit. Special attention has been given to the trapping of the generous greens, which are of a most diversified character: sloping, rolling and punch-bowl. The latest ideas in golf-course construction are embodied in the layout of these up-to-date links and when all is whipped into shape, Brantford golfers will have a testing course of infinite variety." The editor of Canadian Golfer, Ralph Reville, was a member of Brantford.

For 40 years, Brantford members enjoyed this "testing course." In 1960, proposed changes to the clubhouse, curling rink, swimming pool, and other facilities, meant renovating the course. Two-time club president Bruce Forbes,

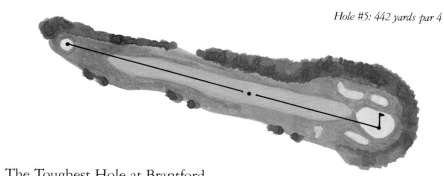

Hole #5: 442 yards par 4

The Toughest Hole at Brantford

Head Professional Jeff Bentley says there's no doubt that the Number 1 stroke hole at Brantford Golf and Country Club is the toughest. "It's a straightaway par-four of 442 yards, but it plays at least 30 yards longer because it's in a low-lying, wet area, so you get very little roll. The second shot is blind: you can see the flag but not the surface of the green. Even after a great drive, you're still hitting in with a long-iron at best. There are three fairway bunkers, a very narrow landing area and trees on both sides. It's a long, tough hole and the only advantage you can get would be to stay up the left side which has a little more elevation."

Since 1879, Brantford Golf and Country Club has moved four times, most recently to this admirable site in 1919.

Brantford Golf and Country Club
Brantford, Ontario

	Length	Par	Rating
Men			
Blue	6612	72	72.5
Red	6358	72	71
Women			
Yellow	5887	75	74.5
White	5703	75	73.5

Hole	Yards	Par
1	511	5
2	334	4
3	173	3
4	526	5
5	442	4
6	353	4
7	355	4
8	156	3
9	308	4
OUT	3158	36
10	168	3
11	408	4
12	476	5
13	458	4
14	508	5
15	192	3
16	458	4
17	154	3
18	530	5
IN	3352	36
Total	6510	72

a Brantford member since 1932, was a close friend of noted Canadian architect C.E. (Robbie) Robinson and approached the designer. "We had no money — and I mean no money," Forbes recalls. "He did it because he was a pal of mine. He never got a cent from us, although he did get a lot of free meals and golf." Forbes is the club's most distinguished member; a fine player and gentleman whose self-admitted "love affair with golf" led to roles as both president and executive-director of the Royal Canadian Golf Association and to eventual nomination to the Canadian Golf Hall of Fame.

Robinson, who had been given his start in

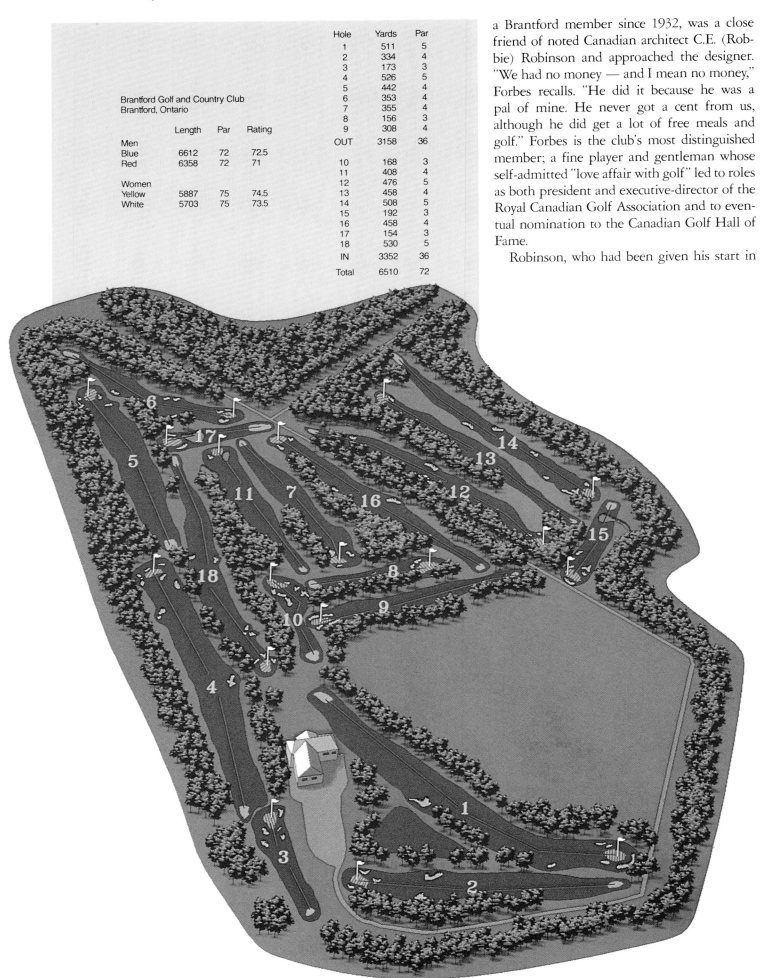

*Another of Brantford's fine par-
threes: the 163-yard 17th.*

the business by Stanley Thompson, summa-
rized his proposals to the board late that year:
"I am now satisfied that I have a well-balanced
series of holes which will eliminate the two
successive par-threes on the second nine and
also provide a strong finishing hole. The
yardage on the first and second nine will be
better balanced and combine into championship length of about 6,800 yards.

"In addition to the new route plan, I would
provide modern designs to replace all present
greens which are small, flat and uninteresting.
Furthermore, they do not provide the shot
values normally called for in present-day golf.
I would also add a modest number of fairway
bunkers which are now lacking on an otherwise
exceptionally fine sequence of golf holes. The
stream would be rerouted and widened to
develop water hazards at strategic points on
two or three holes. All hazards and bunkers
would be placed to test the par golfer but would

be out of range of the average golfer or located
to provide alternate routes for the high-
handicap players. Your club has one of the
finest properties I have inspected, and it is
my opinion that the above architectural refine-
ments will result in a course that will compare
with or surpass the best in Ontario."

The truth of Robinson's prediction has been
proven time and again during the many championships, ranging from junior to senior, and
amateur to professional, held at Brantford in
the intervening years. The first major pro event
held on the redesigned course was the 1970
Canadian PGA Championship, won by Al
Balding of Toronto with a score of 282, six
under par. The course record of 64 was set
by Bob Panasik of Windsor, Ontario, during
the pro-am preceding the tournament. The
Canadian Amateur was held here during Brantford's centennial year of 1979. Rafael Alarcon
of Mexico took the title, also with a 282.

The fourth hole at Essex provides an early challenge — at 459 yards from the blue tees, only the longest hitters have a chance at a par four.

ESSEX

Golf and Country Club

Architect: Donald Ross
Head Professional: Don Harrison
Manager: Larry McKenzie
Superintendent: Stuart Mills

The history of the Essex Golf and Country Club in Windsor, Ontario, dates back almost to the turn of the century and is the result of the grafting of two modest efforts: the Oak Ridge Golf Club and the Walkerville Country Club, rudimentary nine-hole layouts that served the gentry of what would soon become one of the major manufacturing cities of Canada. Coincidentally, the membership of Essex has come traditionally from two sources: Windsor and neighboring Detroit, Michigan, which sits across the Detroit River in the United States.

In 1910, the members of Oak Ridge resolved to purchase land belonging to Colonel Alan Prince, whose descendents continue to belong to Essex. Amalgamating with the Walkerville club (named after millionaire distiller Hiram Walker, who had donated the original land), the newly formed Essex Golf and Country Club opened as nine holes on 40 acres in 1912. An additional 50 acres was added the following year to enable expansion to 18 holes by 1915. That year, more acreage was purchased to lengthen the course to 6,000 yards. Scarcely had this opened for play when the directors, viewing with alarm rising property taxes and the encroachment of the city, decided to instigate a search for more appropriate quarters

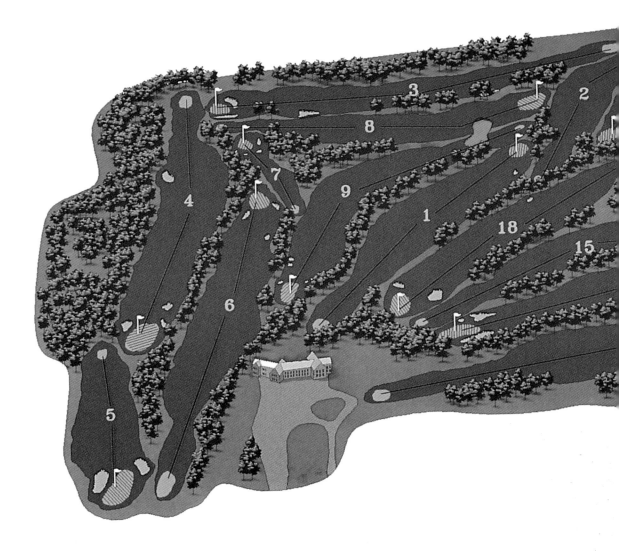

for the golf club. This process was made easier by the ever-widening availability of the automobile, a development which is integrally linked, through good times and bad, with the city of Windsor.

This deliberation took eight years, with the final choice being 126 admirably contoured acres covered with giant oaks, elms and maples. Obviously not ones to make decisions lightly, the directors contacted one of the most prominent and prolific course architects in the world to transform this virgin land into an enviable recreation spot for the upper echelons of Windsor and Detroit society. Donald Ross, originally from Dornoch, Scotland, and schooled by the legendary Tom Morris, was contracted to design the new course. While Ross has been criticized in some quarters for not paying enough personal attention to all his 600-plus creations (indeed, who could?), there is little doubt that the Essex Golf and Country Club was a hands-on project. The

results speak for themselves. Subsequent renovations to drainage systems, tees and bunkers have modernized the course, but have not bastardized Ross's original masterpiece. Although more than 2,000 of the massive elm trees which stood on the land for centuries fell victim to Dutch Elm disease in the 1960s, these have been replaced.

The Tudor-style clubhouse, which opened in 1929, sits low and long at the end of a sweeping driveway. When it was first constructed, the club's historian notes, Ontario was a "dry" province and a bar was not part of the original design. Instead, bedroom-sized cubicles were rented to gentlemen members for entertaining their (male) guests. Furnished with, among other things, a convenient liquor storage cabinet, these compartments remained in the clubhouse until 1959, 30 years after the provincial liquor ban had ended.

This era is also notable for the first mention of Canadian golfing legend Nick Weslock, who

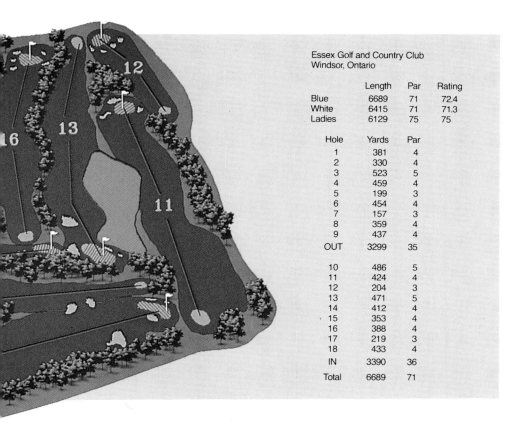

Essex Golf and Country Club			
Windsor, Ontario			
	Length	Par	Rating
Blue	6689	71	72.4
White	6415	71	71.3
Ladies	6129	75	75

Hole	Yards	Par
1	381	4
2	330	4
3	523	5
4	459	4
5	199	3
6	454	4
7	157	3
8	359	4
9	437	4
OUT	3299	35
10	486	5
11	424	4
12	204	3
13	471	5
14	412	4
15	353	4
16	388	4
17	219	3
18	433	4
IN	3390	36
Total	6689	71

One of the shorter par-fours, the eighth hole is very demanding nonetheless.

made his initial appearance at Essex in 1927, caddying at the age of 10 for the famous U.S. professional Walter Hagen. A native of Winnipeg, Weslock's record in amateur play over the intervening years is astounding: multiple Ontario Open and Ontario Amateur wins, many times low amateur in the Canadian Open, numerous international appearance on behalf of Canada. Weslock, still an Essex member, was inducted into the Canadian Golf Hall of Fame in 1971.

The heady days of the club's establishment and entrenchment as "the" club in the border area were deflated in conjunction with the massive unemployment linked with the Great Depression. It was the first indication that the cyclical nature of automobile production, upon which the region depended enormously, could affect the very existence of the Essex Golf and Country Club, despite the fact that automobile magnate Henry Ford was an early member.

These were to be dark days for the club, for many of its members relied, directly or indirectly, on the auto plants for their income. The Depression marked the first of a number of times that Essex would lose members as a result of an economic downturn. Quick and astute financial decisions by the directors have not only saved the club, but placed it on the firm footing it enjoys today.

Although most Canadian golfers have not had the opportunity to play Essex, it stands head and shoulders above most courses in the country by reputation alone. The PGA Tour pros who played it during the 1976 Canadian Open walked away humbled, but anxious to challenge it again. "This course is absolutely mean in tournaments," says Head Professional Don Harrison. "You're fighting it from the time you arrive until the moment you leave.

Enormous bunkers and towering trees await an errant shot on the par-four ninth hole.

And then you say, 'I'll beat it tomorrow.'

"Every time you play Essex, it gets tougher," says Harrison. "After a while, it gets to be a mental game. Essex can beat you many ways, but mostly it's mental. You don't really notice it happening, but you're mentally breaking down. If you don't get it going on the first three holes," he says, "you may be in for a long day." The first two "bonus holes" are short par-fours while the third is a par-five of just over 500 yards. "If you're over par after these three, you're going to be over par for the day, because there just aren't that many chances to get strokes back," says the pro. "The par-fours are either long (from 440 to 470) or they're short with water. They make you work hard and you've got to hit the greens or else.

"This golf course can eat you alive," concludes Harrison. "It's damn tough."

The 1976 Canadian Open

There was much jubiliation in the Essex clubhouse in February 1975 when it was announced that the club would play host to the 1976 Canadian Open, the fourth-oldest national championship in the world. But the announcement was just the first gust in what would turn out to be a whirlwind of controversy. On April 2 (perhaps they were wishing it was a day earlier so the outcome could be written off as a cruel April Fool's joke), the club's directors were informed by the Royal Canadian Golf Association that the invitation to host the Open had been withdrawn due to "the economic conditions in that general geographic market." The RCGA said it feared tournament-related losses to both itself and Essex if the Open was a financial failure and was looking for an alternate site. The RCGA had indeed reaped a whirlwind. Letters flooded into its offices from the mayors of Windsor and Detroit, the United Auto Workers Union, the Golf Association of Michigan and the Chambers of Commerce of Windsor and Detroit. In addition, private citizens wrote the RCGA, pledging substantial sums of money to assure the Open's success, and sportswriters and columnists damned the decision roundly. Awed by the response, the RCGA relented on April 29 and returned the tournament to Essex. More than 90,000 spectators turned up at Essex the following July to watch Tour rookie Jerry Pate, just a month after winning the U.S. Open, claim the title, defeating a field that included Jack Nicklaus, Johnny Miller, Arnold Palmer, Lee Trevino and Gary Player. PGA Tour star Ben Crenshaw has been quoted as saying he enjoyed Essex so much that he wished the Open would be played here every year.

Legendary course architect Donald Ross of Scotland did an exceptional job at Essex.

Perhaps Glen Abbey's most spectacular sight: from the 11th tee, players hit into a river valley some 120 feet below.

GLEN ABBEY

Golf Club

Architect: *Jack Nicklaus*
Head Professional: *Bob Lean*
Manager: *Jack McClellan*
Superintendent: *Dean Baker*

"The shrine of Canadian golf." Perhaps that is putting it a bit strongly, but there is no doubt that Glen Abbey Golf Club is more, much more, than just another public golf course.

The "shrine" phrase first appears in press reports about plans put forth in the early 1970s by the Royal Canadian Golf Association and Great Northern Capital Inc. to develop a permanent site for the Canadian Open, the world's fourth-oldest national championship, hosted by the RCGA. The association's headquarters would be on the site, housing the offices of the people who govern organized amateur golf in this country as well as the Canadian Golf Hall of Fame and Museum.

The religious analogy might have been encouraged not only by the fact that the existing building on the site north of Oakville, Ontario, had been used as a Jesuit retreat, but also by the "golfing god" contracted to design the course: the legendary Jack Nicklaus.

Richard Grimm, now the RCGA's director of professional tournaments, was the organization's president back in 1972 and had acted as chairman of the Open which was held that year at Cherry Hill near Fort Erie, Ontario. When approached by Rod McIsaac of Great Northern, Grimm was leery. "He told me he liked watching the tournament, but it was his feeling that the gallery was not given a fair shake for viewing," Grimm recalled later. "Immediately I thought, 'Here's another gripe from a spectator.' But then he threw me a country mile by saying he had a piece of property in Oakville — and we were thinking about a permanent site. The result of that conversation was meetings with the RCGA, Jack Nicklaus, the Abbey Glen Property Corporation and Imperial Tobacco Limited (longtime sponsors of the Open), and the result of those meetings was Glen Abbey." That "result" has played host to every Canadian Open since 1977, with the exception of 1980 when the national championship was played at Royal Montreal.

When McIsaac made his proposal, more than 200 acres remained of the 350 that mining magnate Andre Dorfman purchased in 1929 to build an imposing castle-like home for himself and his new wife. Sold in 1953 to the

Jesuits, it became available later when Rome ruled that the priests could better serve the church in Toronto. Some of the land was already used for golf, but the layout was unsuitable for the national championship.

Nicklaus, whose professional career was at its peak, had decided to lend his talent to golf course architecture. What he was faced with at Glen Abbey, the first design project he had undertaken on his own, was a schizophrenic situation: most of the land was flat and relatively undistinguished, but the remainder was wonderful river valley land snaking along the meandering Sixteen Mile Creek in the shadow of spectacular bluffs.

More than one million cubic feet of earth were moved to massage the flat land into a fine test of golf, "a panorama of gently rolling fairways," in Nicklaus's words. In excess of 100,000 cubic yards of topsoil became mounds, designed to give spectators at Glen Abbey the

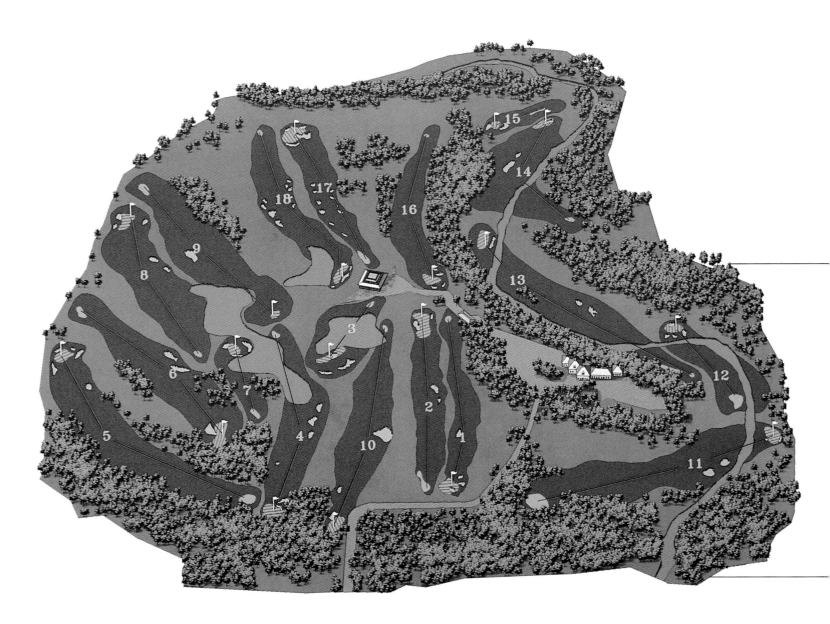

The par-four 14th is considered one of the tougher holes on the PGA Tour.

Glen Abbey Golf Club				Hole	Yards	Par
Oakville, Ontario				1	443	4
				2	414	4
	Length	Par	Rating	3	156	3
Gold	7102	73	75.5	4	417	4
Blue	6618	73	72.5	5	527	5
White	6202	73	70.5	6	437	4
Yellow	5577	74	73.5	7	197	3
				8	433	4
				9	458	4
				OUT	3482	35
				10	435	5
				11	452	4
				12	187	3
				13	529	5
				14	426	4
				15	141	3
				16	516	5
				17	434	4
				18	500	5
				IN	3620	38
				Total	7102	73

"fair shake" McIsaac pined for by acting as natural amphitheatres. "It is the best spectator course in the world," the designer said upon its completion in 1976. But it is the five holes along the creek, the "valley holes" kickstarted by a drive off the 11th tee into a gorge some 120 feet below, that burn themselves into the memories of competitors and spectators alike. These holes have the reputation of being one of the toughest stretches on the entire PGA Tour.

The 11th fairway, squeezed by trees on the left and bunkers on the right, ends abruptly. For at that point, Sixteen Mile Creek, ill-named because it is closer to a river in nature and has been known to tear out bridges when swollen by rain, flows across the hole. On the other side of the creek, the undulating green awaits, well bunkered and tucked in at the base of those towering bluffs. The waterway comes into play again on the par-three 12th, twice on the 13th (passing in front of the tee, continuing down the left boundary and then slicing back in front of the green, daring you to go for the long, narrow green in two shots) and on the par-four 14th, where it has claimed many a sliced drive. This has traditionally been one of the toughest holes on the course for the PGA Tour pros, with the stroke average approaching 4.5 some years. That average is inflated not only by the presence of the creek, but also by the swale that cuts through the centre of the rolling green, making three-putts commonplace.

While Glen Abbey can stretch up to 7,100 yards for the Canadian Open, the only PGA Tour event held outside the United States, a variety of tee positions offer distances right down to 5,200. "I regard the emphasis on length and huge greens as the two worst faults of modern golf course design," said Nicklaus. "Many people assume my golf courses will be long monsters, but I consider golf to be a game of precision, not strength." To his credit, Nicklaus kept in mind that the PGA Tour is at Glen Abbey for but one week each year. The rest of the 30,000 rounds are played by public golfers.

Nicklaus and Glen Abbey are linked in one more way, apparently for all time: Of all his Tour victories, 70 in total, none is a Canadian Open. He has been the runner-up an unbelievable seven times.

The slick greens at Glen Abbey, like the 12th, are among the best in the country.

From the fourteenth green, Glen Abbey ascends from the spectacular river valley.

How The Pros Play Glen Abbey

For Dave Barr, the veteran PGA Tour pro from British Columbia, one key to success at Glen Abbey is the left-to-right shot. Barr, who has finished as high as fourth in the Canadian Open here, believes the two toughest holes on the course are eight and nine. On the eighth, he tries to play down the left side beside the two bunkers, which leaves an open shot to the green with a long-iron. The key to the ninth, a long par-four, is keeping the ball in the fairway. "If you end up in the (right-side) bunker, you have to play a 210-yard sand shot," he said prior to the 1990 Open. Ironically, it was in that very situation that he found himself during the final round of the tournament. Taking only a minute amount of sand on the downswing with his two-iron meant a "fat" shot that found the pond some 50 yards short of the green. The resulting triple-bogey took him out of contention.

When he plays the Abbey, Barr believes he will score well if he can get through holes eight to 11 in even-par. The 13th hole, a 529-yard par-five, can be reached with two mighty blows. "I usually won't go for it unless I'm 220 yards or less from the green," says Barr, who has won more than $1 million on the pro tours.

On both 14, the 426-yard par-four, and 15, a par-three of 141 yards, the severe slope of the green means keeping the ball below the hole is a necessity. "The key to 16 is staying in the fairway," says Barr of the 516-yard par-five. "You can usually reach it in two from either side of the fairway. There's a good chance for a birdie here."

The 17th hole again favors a fade to stay away from the deep bunkers on the left. A good tee shot is rewarded with a short-iron approach. The 18th, a 500-yard par-five, has been called one of the great finishing holes. It tempts players to go for the green in two, but taunts them with a large pond in front of the long, narrow green. Three of the last six holes at the Abbey are par-fives, a situation that has made for some exciting conclusions to past Canadian Opens.

The East Course at Hamilton Golf and Country Club is the newest of the three nines, but is comparable to the original 18 in design and challenge.

———— *Ancaster, Ontario* ————

HAMILTON

Golf and Country Club

*Architect: Harry Colt (18)
and C.E. Robinson (9)
Head Professional: Rob McDannold
Manager: John Mickle
Superintendent: Rod Trainor*

Driving up to the stately, ivy-enveloped mansion which serves as the clubhouse for the Hamilton Golf and Country Club, even the most jaded golfer realizes that here is something extraordinary. The quiet, superlative elegance of both the course and the club is seldom matched anywhere in the world of golf.

The Hamilton Golf and Country Club was once located in the city of Hamilton, on the present site of the Hamilton Centre Mall, when it was founded in 1894. A couple of years later, yielding to the pressures of urban growth and accompanying tax pressures as many city courses did in those days, the club moved to acreage on the side of Hamilton Mountain. This location, now the Chedoke municipal course, served the membership until 1913 when the club's fathers decided to build 18 holes and an imposing clubhouse farther up the face of Hamilton Mountain, where the topography and view were unequalled.

Harry Colt, riding the success of his acclaimed new course at England's Sunningdale and the Toronto Golf Club, was contracted to design the layout. Drawing on his British heritage, he crafted a fine bump-and-run course which officially opened in 1916. At Sunningdale, Colt gave a hint of what would eventually be

one of his great contributions to golf course architecture: comprehensive tree-planting programs.

The site of Hamilton Golf and Country Club, which now covers more than 300 acres, was largely farmer's fields when the course was designed, a situation unimaginable to a present-day visitor. In the mind of present Head Professional Rob McDannold, Colt's visionary genius is unsurpassed: "When you look at the original map of this property, there were almost no trees. Now it looks as if it was carved out of the forest. Colt planned it so there are exact gaps in the trees for sunlight, for the wind, for shots. He had an absolutely amazing ability to foresee what this course would look like 50 years later. The trees look like they've been here forever."

An immediate success upon its opening, the Hamilton Golf and Country Club played host to the Canadian Open just three years later. The first national championship played after the end of the First World War, it drew more than usual interest for a number of reasons, not the least of which was the fact that it

Surrounded by forest and dotted with ponds and streams, Hamilton is a shotmaker's delight.

counted the great U.S. amateur Bobby Jones among the field. But Jones could do no better than a tie with Ottawa's Karl Keffer for second, as Douglas Edgar of Atlanta, Georgia, won the first of his two consecutive Open titles. Edgar's four-round total of 278 was at that time the world record for professionals. The second, and final, time the club opened its course to the Open, in 1930, Tommy Armour of Detroit defeated fellow PGA Tour pro Leo Diegel in a 36-hole playoff. To get into the playoff, Armour had to craft a stunning 64 in the final round, a course record that stands today. Jim Nelford of Vancouver tied it in the 1977 Canadian Amateur, but did not translate that into a victory, finishing second to Rod Spittle of Niagara Falls, Ontario.

Playing the original 18 holes (the West and South nines) today can be very reminiscent of those early days when Jones and Armour trod Hamilton's fairways, for an astute membership has taken care to maintain the original design in large part. The rolling fairways are separated by those now-mature trees and the design is as valuable and serviceable as a fine

Hamilton Golf and Country Club
Ancaster, Ontario

West Nine	Length	Par	Rating
Blue	3283	35	N/A
White	3142	35	N/A
Red	2958	35	N/A
Yellow	2885	37	N/A
South Nine			
Blue	3291	35	N/A
White	3114	35	N/A
Red	2845	35	N/A
Yellow	2878	37	N/A
East Nine			
Blue	3259	35	N/A
White	3051	35	N/A
Red	2886	35	N/A
Yellow	2811	37	N/A

West Course Hole	Yards	Par	South Course			East Course		
1	416	4	1	345	4	1	396	4
2	431	4	2	442	4	2	420	4
3	396	4	3	380	4	3	383	4
4	525	5	4	209	3	4	392	4
5	316	4	5	395	4	5	196	3
6	208	3	6	378	4	6	422	4
7	373	4	7	183	3	7	156	3
8	193	3	8	529	5	8	522	5
9	425	4	9	429	4	9	372	4
Total	3283	35	Total	3291	35	Total	3259	35

antique. Colt, the first golf course architect who was not a professional golfer, nonetheless has managed to provide a fine test of golf. With only two par-fives, this beautifully conditioned 6,600-yard layout plays much longer than the card indicates.

While the course is not overly tight, well-positioned tee shots are vital to a respectable score. The majority of the par-fours require good planning and execution to prepare for the most advantageous approach to the green. Straying into the stands of mature hardwoods seldom means a lost ball, but those massive trees will no doubt prevent advancing it once found. The par-threes at Hamilton are strong: all but one play to more than 180 yards from the blue tees and more than 175 from the whites.

"The first four holes can make or break you," says McDannold. "It's a very difficult start. The first two holes are par-fours of more than 400 yards. Your first drive has to be about 240 yards into the prevailing wind to the corner of the dogleg. You can't cut the corner, unless you can hit it at least 270, because the corner is filled with hills, valleys, pot bunkers and so on. So you have to play right, even though that gives you a longer shot in to a well-bunkered green. Number 2 is a dogleg-right, with bunkers right and trees left, that requires a long, accurate drive. The green has lots of bunkers and you're dealing with that wind again as you hit anything from a two- to a five-iron in.

"The third hole demands another accurate drive, but no more than 235 yards, otherwise you'll be down a steep slope covered with rough. Hit a long-iron off the tee, and you'll have about 165 in to an elevated green with a shelf. Don't be long on this one. The fourth hole can give you a bit of a reprieve if you hit it straight off the tee. In a tournament, I wouldn't hit driver off the tee here. There's a pit left, so stay a little right, but notice the trees and fairway bunkers down that side. This hole is reachable, but there's so many opportunities to get into trouble that I would just accept it being a three-shot hole and try to get close with that third shot. The green is long, narrow and elevated, bunkered left and front."

In 1975, the growing membership was placing an enormous burden on Colt's 18 holes, so the decision was made to bring in noted Canadian architect C.E. (Robbie) Robinson to design an additional nine holes of a complementary nature. "The East nine is spectacular," enthuses McDannold. "It's very tight; a great members' course."

It should be noted that Nicol Thompson, elder brother of talented course architect Stanley Thompson, served as the head professional at the Hamilton Golf and Country Club for 50 years until his retirement in 1945. He was succeeded by Dick Borthwick (1946-74), Ken Steeves (1975-80), Gary Maue (1981-89) and McDannold.

The third hole on the West Course requires an iron off the tee and a mid-iron to hold the elevated green.

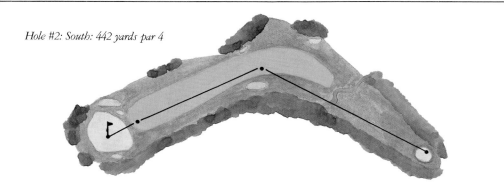

Hole #2: South: 442 yards par 4

The greens at Hamilton are not overly large, but are subtle and fast.

The Toughest Hole at Hamilton

"The second hole on our South course is the toughest of our 27," says Hamilton Head Professional Rob McDannold, "and I think it's one of the very best in Canada." Playing 442 yards from the blue tees and 406 from the whites, this hole demands a 230-yard drive to the corner of the dogleg-left. The mature stand of trees in the corner deters long-ball hitters from trying to carry the dogleg. McDannold suggests a three-wood off the tee, since a driver might carry the ball through the fairway. "From there, it's all uphill into the wind to an elevated green with a steep bunker right and trees, a slope and rough left," says the pro. "I tell most people to play up short of the green on their second shot and play it as a par-five; it saves them a lot of grief."

The rolling, wooded acreage of London Hunt is ideal for riding to the hounds or hunting birdies.

LONDON

Hunt and Country Club

Architect: Robert Trent Jones
Head Professional: Ken Girard
Manager: John Franz
Superintendent: John Bennett

The year 1904 was an auspicious one for the founding of a golf club in Canada: the first Canadian Open was held at Royal Montreal, and George S. Lyon won the Olympic gold medal in golf. Although golf was the latest addition to London Hunt's portfolio, the club itself had been firmly established for many years. Informally, the practice of gathering for the social and sporting aspects of the hunt dated back to the 1830s when a British garrison was established here in the wake of the Rebellion of 1837. By 1885, the need for a more organized association was felt and the precursor of today's London Hunt and Country Club was founded.

Now situated on about 300 acres on the Thames River in the heart of London, London Hunt is a refuge from the harsh realities of the outside world for its 1,800 members. Aside from the splendid golf course designed by Robert Trent Jones in 1960, the club prides itself on having a variety of activities to involve people of all ages and interests. Aside from the more mundane pursuits such as tennis and swimming, members have access to trapshooting and, on Wednesdays and Saturdays, they can still ride to the hounds.

Although golf was not initially the first priority, the members took to the game willingly and prided themselves on their course

London Hunt, a Robert Trent Jones design, is notable for its huge greens.

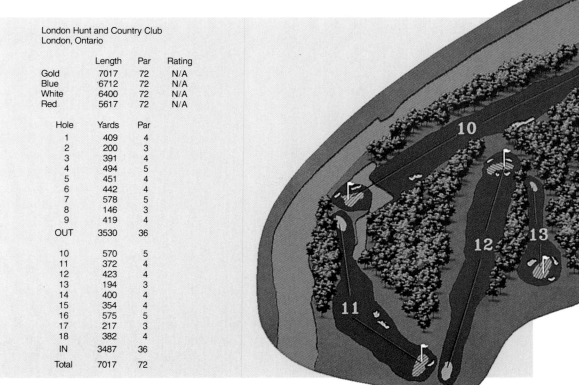

London Hunt and Country Club
London, Ontario

	Length	Par	Rating
Gold	7017	72	N/A
Blue	6712	72	N/A
White	6400	72	N/A
Red	5617	72	N/A

Hole	Yards	Par
1	409	4
2	200	3
3	391	4
4	494	5
5	451	4
6	442	4
7	578	5
8	146	3
9	419	4
OUT	3530	36
10	570	5
11	372	4
12	423	4
13	194	3
14	400	4
15	354	4
16	575	5
17	217	3
18	382	4
IN	3487	36
Total	7017	72

in the early part of the 20th Century. The club history, written on the occasion of London Hunt's centennial in 1985, recounts that the golf links of the early days, although considerably shorter than the present course, were quite challenging and were located on land leased from the University of Western Ontario. "The fairways were narrow: one visitor described his round 'like playing 5th Avenue.' There were few bunkers, but the terrain was tricky. Steep inclines and sharp declivities, massive elms (before the advent of Dutch Elm disease) and maples, as well as the Medway Creek, formed natural barriers. After the mid-1920s, manoeuvring around new university buildings posed an additional hazard. It was easy to go out of bounds, to richocet wildly off a tree or find oneself on the brism (a local term for 'brink of a chasm'). Successful play

requested that they leave so he could play his round undisturbed. It was not the last time that London Hunt witnessed some unusual golf, the club history notes. In the 1954 Americas Cup, "the drive of an intrepid Mexican competitor landed on the flat roof of the clubhouse. Undaunted, he went out onto the roof from a bedroom window, played a wedge shot to the green and holed out in two putts for a par four." The Americas Cup, a team competition between Canada, Mexico and the United States, was won that year by the Americans by one point over the Canadian side captained by London Hunt member Jack Nash.

In 1960, renowned U.S. architect Robert Trent Jones was contracted to build a course commensurate with the reputation of the London Hunt and Country Club. For Head Pro-

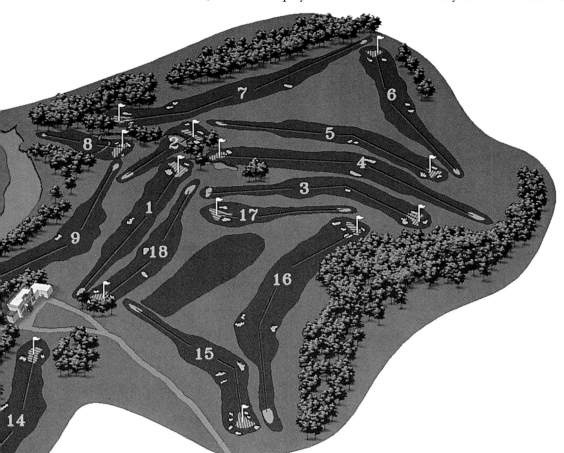

called for use of every club in the bag and particular skill with irons."

This was the site visited by the Prince of Wales in 1919. Showing that golf is the great leveller, the Prince refused a request by a photographer from the local newspaper to pose in a golfing stance by saying: "Well, no, I really can't. And the reason I must refuse is that I play so poor a game." Shaken by the presence of the spectators who followed him, he

fessional Ken Girard, a taste of playing the layout during the 1970 Canadian Open was enough to make him want to return as an employee when the job was offered in 1972. He is an unabashed fan of both the club with its family atmosphere as well as the course itself.

"What makes this course unique is the extremely large greens," says Girard. "They are absolutely huge. For example, the 10th green is 100 yards long — that's a five-club difference when you're hitting into it. If you're 150 yards out, you can hit a nine-iron to the front of the green or a five-iron to the back. On these greens, it's not a matter of hitting the green, it's a matter of hitting the right quadrant of the green. The category 'Greens in regulation' means nothing here. In fact, often you'd rather be off the green and chipping instead of having a 250-foot putt." To be fair, the greens do not resemble the Himalayas. Instead, these spacious putting surfaces are gently rolling, putting the emphasis on a precise approach shot. In any case, don't leave your approach short: In true Robert Trent Jones' style, danger lurks in front of the greens in the shape of deep bunkers.

The 14th green is presided over by the elegant clubhouse.

The 10th hole, with its 100-yard-long green, has been singled out in the past as being one of the best golf holes in Canada. It certainly stands out in the memory of anyone who has been fortunate enough to play London Hunt. From the back tee, this par-five stretches almost

600 yards through bush on both sides. The Thames River guards the entire right boundary, while a pond threatens a wayward tee shot. The green is surrounded by water. "This is a true three-shotter," says Girard.

The toughest hole on the course, which can play as long as 7,000 yards from the longest of its five sets of tees, is the sixth, says the pro, who holds the course record of 65 along with four other players. "It's a long par-four that plays about 440 from the back. You hit down into the valley and then up to an elevated green with bunkers in front. It's a drive and a long-iron at least."

London Hunt has a long history of accomplished players, including the legendary Sandy Somerville. Included on that list must be the diminutive Ed Ervasti, who in his stellar amateur career has claimed titles across North America. Still going strong in 1990, Ervasti fired a stunning 63 at age 76 from the forward tees at London Hunt.

C. Ross (Sandy) Somerville

In many ways Charles Ross (Sandy) Somerville personified the quiet elegance of the London Hunt and Country Club. Restrained and self-effacing, Somerville managed to compile an almost unparalleled amateur golf record in the first half of the 20th Century. The native of London, Ontario, played in 18 Canadian Amateurs, winning six; 14 U.S. Amateurs, winning once (1932); and three British Amateurs, making it to the semi-finals in 1938. He also recorded the first hole-in-one at the Masters, in 1934. Tim Wharnsby, writing in SCORE magazine, recounts a conversation with Somerville in 1990: "On the day he returned from his U.S. Amateur victory, London city officials had a small reception planned to honor the new champion in downtown London. Instead, Somerville had a couple of trusted friends pick him up at the train station in nearby St. Thomas. They drove into London the back way, straight to Somerville's small downtown apartment where he lived with his mother." His accomplishments merited him a well-deserved place in the Canadian Golf Hall of Fame.

London Hunt is as picturesque as it is challenging.

METROPOLITAN TORONTO

Board of Trade Country Club

Architect: Howard Watson
Head Professional: Michael Schurman
Manager: David Fairley
Superintendent: Gordon Witteveen

Half an hour north of Toronto sprawls a 45-hole country club unique in the world. The Metropolitan Toronto Board of Trade Country Club is the only golf course owned by a Board of Trade or Chamber of Commerce, says General Manager David Fairley. "The Board of Trade is a policy/advocacy group for business," he says, noting that it's not the kind of group with which you immediately associate the ownership of a golf course. The Board is the largest in the world with 17,000 members.

To their credit, the Board in 1963 decided to assemble more than 300 acres in the rolling, wooded hills of Woodbridge to build a place where the business community could play golf and have tournaments. Since the trendy golfing phrase these days is "Golf is the sport of business," then that 1963 Board deserves full marks for foresight. "On a fine summer day, I'm sure there's as much business done on this course as there is in many offices downtown," says Fairley.

Although Canadian businessmen have a reputation for being cautious, the decision to build the Board of Trade Country Club involved a significant amount of risk. That move has paid off handsomely as the more than 1,600 golfing members play tens

of thousands of rounds annually on the 45 holes. The Board made a shrewd decision as well in its choice of personnel: architect Howard Watson and Head Professional Murray Tucker.

Watson, who served as president of the American Society of Golf Course Architects in 1958, learned his trade at the hand of none other than Stanley Thompson, the dean of Canadian course architects. Thompson hired Watson in 1929 to work on the construction of the Royal York course in Toronto (later renamed St. George's). Impressed with the young man, Thompson sent him to work with his U.S. partner, Robert Trent Jones. In this way, Watson drew on two of the premier design geniuses of the 20th Century, and his admirable creation of both the West and East courses

at Board of Trade reflect their influences.

Tucker, eventually awarded the distinction of Master Professional by the Canadian Professional Golfers' Association, was "the man" at the Board of Trade Country Club from 1965 until his retirement in 1989.

"Howard had his job, which was to build the different courses," recalls Tucker, "and I had mine, which was to get people around them. I remember asking him about the design and he told me that the object was to build something that would still be considered modern 40 or 50 years hence. I think he did that. The West course, especially, is really excellent and throws some changes at you because of the wind."

The West course is widely considered the superior layout, although a composite of its

"A great par-three." The 186-yard third hole on the West Course.

holes, and some from the East course, have been used during notable competitions held here. The 1986 du Maurier Ltd. Classic was played on the West, with the 18th hole of the East becoming the finishing hole. Pat Bradley won the event in a playoff over Ayako Okamoto after the two tied at 12-under 276, an LPGA record for 72 holes. The 1967 Carling World Championship, won by Billy Casper in

a playoff over Al Geiberger, used a combination of holes as well. To achieve the West's stature, Watson set tees and greens on natural promontories and took full advantage of the Humber River, which wanders through the lower acreage. The river comes into play on five of the West's first nine holes, while trees mark the back nine.

The opening hole on the West course is

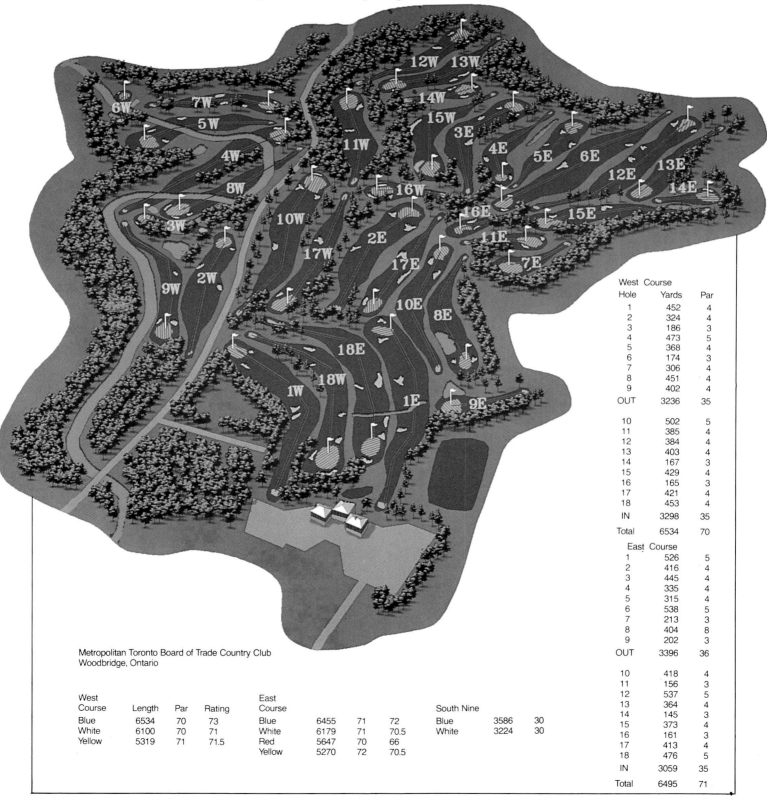

Metropolitan Toronto Board of Trade Country Club
Woodbridge, Ontario

West Course	Yards	Par
1	452	4
2	324	4
3	186	3
4	473	5
5	368	4
6	174	3
7	306	4
8	451	4
9	402	4
OUT	3236	35
10	502	5
11	385	4
12	384	4
13	403	4
14	167	3
15	429	4
16	165	3
17	421	4
18	453	4
IN	3298	35
Total	6534	70

East Course	Yards	Par
1	526	5
2	416	4
3	445	4
4	335	4
5	315	4
6	538	5
7	213	3
8	404	8
9	202	3
OUT	3396	36
10	418	4
11	156	3
12	537	5
13	364	4
14	145	3
15	373	4
16	161	3
17	413	4
18	476	5
IN	3059	35
Total	6495	71

West Course	Length	Par	Rating
Blue	6534	70	73
White	6100	70	71
Yellow	5319	71	71.5

East Course			
Blue	6455	71	72
White	6179	71	70.5
Red	5647	70	66
Yellow	5270	72	70.5

South Nine		
Blue	3586	30
White	3224	30

The par-four fifth hole on the West Course features a little of every sort of hazard.

a dogleg-left that plays into the prevailing wind and demands a tee shot of 250 yards to carry fairway bunkers on the left and to avoid the out-of-bounds that runs down the entire left side. The huge, undulating and very quick green is characteristic of the Board of Trade. Number 3 is "a great par-three," says Tucker. "It plays about 187 over a pond, with a nice tree on the right. You can get into trouble if you're long and you pull the ball, because the river can come into play. A very honest and pretty hole."

The fourth hole is the Number 1 stroke hole, a 479-yard par-five from the back tees. "This is a great driving hole," says Tucker. "You've got to crack it about 260 or 270 over the Humber River, which comes across again about 40 yards in front of the green. There's bush on both sides, but this can be a birdie hole." Number 6 is another good par-three, but don't over-protect against the pond to the right of the green. Nancy White, a Canadian playing on the LPGA Tour, found that out the hard way during the du Maurier Ltd. Classic. Playing well, she pulled her tee shot on this hole and it found the river on the left, resulting

in a triple-bogey. Ignore the pond and the fact that the green slopes down to it, advises the longtime pro, "the high fade is the shot here."

The best hole on the golf course, in Tucker's opinion, is the eighth, a herculean par-four that plays even longer than the 451 yards on the card. "This is a great hole. It's a slight dogleg-right and the best drive is a slight draw down the middle. You'll be hitting anything from a three-iron to a seven-iron from there. The green is small and very severely trapped and is built to receive shots from the left side of the fairway."

Tucker calls the ninth hole a "strategic" hole. The dogleg-right features the Humber River down the entire right side and a pond on the left. While the best local strategy is to hit the driver and draw the ball into the fairway from the river, Tucker says there have been other schools of thought. "Gary Player was here for the Carling World and he said the way to play this hole was two-iron and then a four- or five-iron," Tucker recalls. "Well, he double-bogeyed this hole and missed the playoff by a shot."

The back nine provides little respite for

Real Winter Rules

Gordon Witteveen, the outstanding course superintendent at the Metropolitan Toronto Board of Trade Country Club, is nothing if not innovative and imaginative. In order to satisfy the rabid golfers at his club, he decided to allow the club's executive-length, nine-hole layout — which he had designed — to remain open year-round. Blowing the snow off the tees and greens of the par-threes as well as from the fairways of the par-fours provided the opportunity. On some days in January and February, there are 50 or 60 players trudging through snow to play golf with orange balls. The one-day record is 150. The course doesn't suffer from the exposure, Witteveen says, adding with a proud smile, "We've had holes-in-one every month of the year!"

anyone who hasn't brought their "A" game and doesn't employ sound course management. The 18th hole is a strong finishing hole. The object on the dogleg-right is to clear the hill in the landing area without carrying right through the fairway. The second shot is up an imposing hill to a punitive green; "it can be a nightmare if you're above the hole," says Tucker.

Tucker's final analysis: "To score well at the Board of Trade Country Club, you must hit great approaches or great putts. This course gives you nothing; don't expect the ball to run into the hole on its own."

The East Course is no slouch. Here, the 427-yard par-four 17th hole.

MISSISSAUGUA

Golf and Country Club

Architect: George Cumming
Head Professional: Gar Hamilton
Manager: Walter Haselsteiner
Superintendent: Paul White

Rarely in the course of any human endeavor is there one such single symbolic moment as is evident in the founding of the Mississaugua Golf and Country Club.

As recounted in the club's history, written to salute its 75th anniversary in 1981, the scene was set when a group of enthusiastic members of the Highlands Golf Club, which was about to fall victim to development, were travelling in a surrey down a dirt road which paralleled the Credit River west of Toronto. It was the autumn of 1905 and their mission was to find a new golfing home well removed from the city.

"The day was warm and the road was dusty," the chronicle notes. "When the men spotted a couple of fruit trees, they halted the surrey to pick some apples. On impulse, John Hall jumped a low fence and strode across a broad meadow. He gazed in astonishment at the beautiful scene down the valley, then turned to his friends and shouted, 'We've found it!'

" 'Found what?' they shouted back. 'Why, our golf course, of course!' Hall replied.

"Hall returned to the surrey and, impulsively pulling a golf club from his bag, picked up a ball and went back to the top of the

The 417-yard par four 8th hole features a tight green protected by sand and trees.

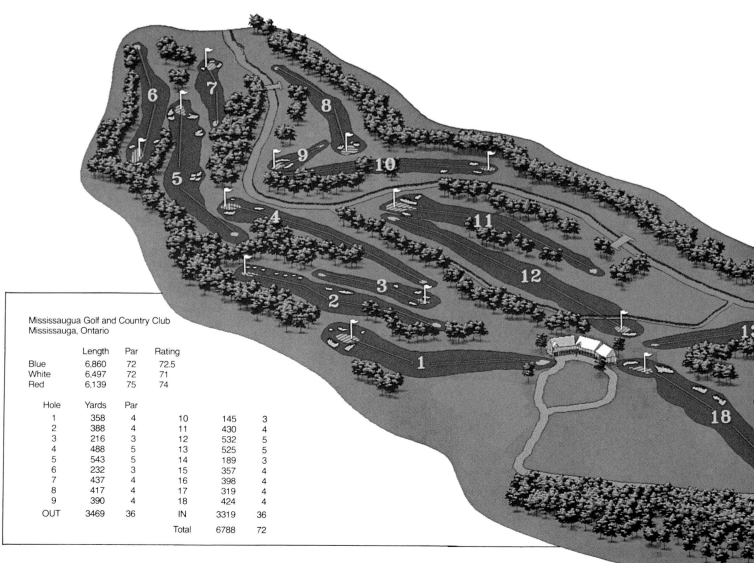

Mississaugua Golf and Country Club
Mississauga, Ontario

	Length	Par	Rating
Blue	6,860	72	72.5
White	6,497	72	71
Red	6,139	75	74

Hole	Yards	Par			
1	358	4	10	145	3
2	388	4	11	430	4
3	216	3	12	532	5
4	488	5	13	525	5
5	543	5	14	189	3
6	232	3	15	357	4
7	437	4	16	398	4
8	417	4	17	319	4
9	390	4	18	424	4
OUT	3469	36	IN	3319	36
			Total	6788	72

hill. He teed up, swung his brassie and drove the ball far into the valley below."

With such fervor, moulded in the heat generated by the discovery of such an awesome setting, the founders overlooked such picayune details as the fact that the course was all but inaccessible to the transportation modes of that era and that a wealthy, enthusiastic membership had to be raised. All such apparent obstacles were successfully dealt with in turn.

The club was extremely fortunate in having as its first president, Lauchlan Alexander Hamilton, land commissioner of the Canadian Pacific Railway. Among his feats was the surveying and laying out of the city of Vancouver. The club archives make this assessment: "He laid out the City of Vancouver and then devoted the rest of his career to the making of the Mississaugua Golf Club." Hamilton was president for 10 years and, by the time he retired, the lovely Tudor-style clubhouse had been completed and the club was settled and prosperous.

George Cumming, the noted professional at the Toronto Golf Club and 1905 Canadian Open champion, was responsible for Mississaugua's initial layout in 1906 with the assistance of Percy Barrett, professional at Toronto's Lambton club. In 1909, Cumming was commissioned to revamp the course. Famed architect Donald Ross of Dornoch, Scotland, and Pinehurst, North Carolina, toured the course 10 years later, making recommendations to change bunkering and lengthen holes. Thus, by 1923, the course had been all but rebuilt. Apart from changes in 1928, 1958 and the late 1980s, the course has not changed sub-

stantially since. From its opening holes on the bluffs overlooking the serpentine Credit River, it swoops down into the valley where John Hall drove his ball in 1905. Snaking along the valley, it loops back and forth across the river before wending its way back up the precipitous bank.

Mississaugua's physical attributes are as enviable as the unequalled calibre of its membership. In its early years, it was home to "Canada's premier golfing family" — the Thompson brothers. Bill, Stanley and Frank were the Mississaugua contingent of the five brothers. Nicol was the eldest, a professional who played out of the Hamilton Golf and Country Club in nearby Ancaster, Ontario. Matt lived and worked in the golf trade in Manitoba. The first record of their achievements came in 1919 when the three amateurs finished one, two and three in the first Toronto and District Golf Tournament to be held after the war. Frank and Bill went on to capture many tournaments including national amateur titles. Stanley, while a formidable player, would make his mark as one of the most esteemed golf course architects in the world. Indeed, he would redesign and lengthen the Mississaugua course in later years.

Although several Toronto-area courses can make a legitimate claim to Ada Mackenzie, this Canadian golfing legend took up the game by hitting balls at the Mississaugua course at the age of 17. Both during and after her time at Mississaugua, she would make an indelible mark on the game in this country, leading to her induction into the Canadian Golf Hall of Fame. When she died in 1973 at the age of 81, Ada Mackenzie had won almost every major tournament at home and abroad, including five Canadian Ladies' Opens and five Canadian Close championships, eight Canadian Ladies' Seniors Golf Association Championships and two Ontario Seniors titles. In 1933, she won every major ladies' golf championship in Canada and was named the outstanding female athlete in the country.

Tradition is a Mississaugua byword, and no mention of the club would be complete without discussing the contribution of Gordon Brydson, head professional from 1932 to 1971 and an honorary life member since. He was a fine tournament player, winning the Canadian PGA Championship, two Ontario Opens and the Quebec Open, but it is for his unstinting contribution to the life of "his" club that he is revered. "Mississaugua has been my second home," he has said. And the sentiment is reciprocated, as one longtime member stated

Hole #12: 532 yards par 5

More cautious players lay up in front of the river with their second shot on the par-five 13th.

The Big Chief Factor

In addition to numerous other tournaments, Mississaugua Golf and Country Club has played host to six Canadian Open Championships: 1931 (Walter Hagen), 1938 (Sam Snead), 1942 (Craig Wood), 1951 (Jim Ferrier), 1965 (Gene Littler) and 1974 (Bobby Nichols). It is safe to say that in every tournament round, the par-five 12th hole, nicknamed the Big Chief, has played a role. It was the site of spectacular play in 1938 during a playoff between eventual winner Sam Snead and Harry Cooper. Snead's second shot was a five-wood which hit a spectator and bounced onto the green, 35 feet from the hole. Cooper was off the green in two and chipped to 25 feet. Snead, trailing by one shot, putted for his eagle while Cooper rolled in the birdie putt. In 1965, Jack Nicklaus came to grief on this hole when his second shot cleared the river, but came to rest on the side of the plateau on which the green sits. Carding a bogey instead of an eagle or even birdie or par, it has been said, "cost Nicklaus the Open." He lost to Gene Littler by one shot in what might have been considered an omen. Of all his titles, the Canadian Open eluded Nicklaus for his entire career.

at Brydson's 80th birthday party in 1987: "Gordie has been Mississaugua; that's all there is to it."

Present Head Professional Gar Hamilton, an ideal successor to Brydson in many aspects, says Mississaugua is "an outstanding old course that is often underrated." He points to back-to-back par-fives on the back nine that typify the course's toughness.

"This course is very difficult," says Hamilton, "because it never lets up; it's relentless. The middle of the course is key to a good scoring round. Number 12 is an old hole, the par-five Big Chief. The temptation there is to go for the green in two, but you've got to hit your second shot to a small, elevated green over the river. Not a high-percentage shot for most players . . .

"The 13th is a very difficult par-five as well. The fairway slopes quite a bit, leaving a small landing area if you want to try to get home with two shots. You'll need two absolutely perfect shots to get home here; anything less leaves you with a poor lie. In fact, many players lay up in front of the river on their second shot, just to make sure."

By the way, if you're wondering why the golf club's name is spelled differently than the city's name, there's no good reason, says the club's history. In the 1940s, "the club changed the spelling of its name from Mississauga (which corresponded with both the name of the Mississauga Indians, whose heritage was associated with the land, and the club's address on Mississauga Road) to Mississaugua, which corresponds, historically, with nothing at all." No one has been able to determine the logic behind the change in the years since.

No. 10, a short par-three, requires hitting over the Credit River, a recurring hazard at Mississaugua.

A small lake guards the 17th and 18th fairways, making the National's finishing holes among the most difficult in Canada.

—————— *Woodbridge, Ontario* ——————

THE NATIONAL

Golf Club

Architects: Tom and George Fazio
Director of Golf: Ben Kern
Superintendent: John Cherry

The National. To those who know this course, consistently rated the toughest in Canada, no two words inspire the same respect or, in some cases, fear.

The National Golf Club was opened in 1974, the culmination of a dream held by businessman Gil Blechman. "I wanted to build the best course in the world; a U.S. Open-type course," Blechman says. He enlisted Tom and George Fazio, two of the world's premier course architects, to build the best possible layout on the 400 acres he had assembled in the rolling hills north of Woodbridge, Ontario.

They were more than equal to the task. Lee Trevino, who won the 1979 Canadian Professional Golfers' Association Championship here, still calls it one of his favorite courses in the world. It is a note of distinction for The National that Trevino's winning score was 285 — one over par. Perhaps the one true mark of a great course is that it is never humbled; not even by the best.

"Everyone always talks about how difficult and hard the golf course is," says Blechman, who sold the course to the members in 1987, "but it is only the odd person who really appreciates its terrible beauty. You literally get seduced going around the bend from No. 10 to No. 13, and it's continually building to a crescendo until you come to 17 and 18."

It has been said that the first three holes of The National lure the unwary, the unprepared and the high-handicapper into a false sense of security. The opening tee shot is invited down a comfortably sloped fairway; if you stay slightly left off the tee, hitting the well-protected green should be only a short-iron situation. The second hole is a straightaway par-four, and the third another downhill par-four with an emphasis on the second shot into a green guarded on the left by a pond and on the right by bunkers. The good player may well be at even par when stepping onto the fourth tee. A humbling experience awaits.

The fourth hole is the toughest on the course, a tortuous par-five that may send the wayward hitter to the fifth tee smarting from a double-bogey. And that is just a glimpse of what lies ahead. The next hole, the first par-three you encounter, is 180 yards from the blue tees, generally into the wind to a green encircled by bunkers. Err to the left, since a slice will route your ball down a hillside and onto the fourth fairway.

As windswept and open as the front nine may be, the trip home is shorter, narrower, heavily wooded, and sports water in play on all nine holes. A river valley some 100 feet lower than the front nine provides the routing for some of the most difficult holes in Canada. Your initiation to the back nine is dramatic. The tee for the par-three 10th hole is high on a bluff, while the green awaits in the valley far below. Club selection and a smooth swing are vital here, since danger lurks in the form of rough in front, a pond right and a huge

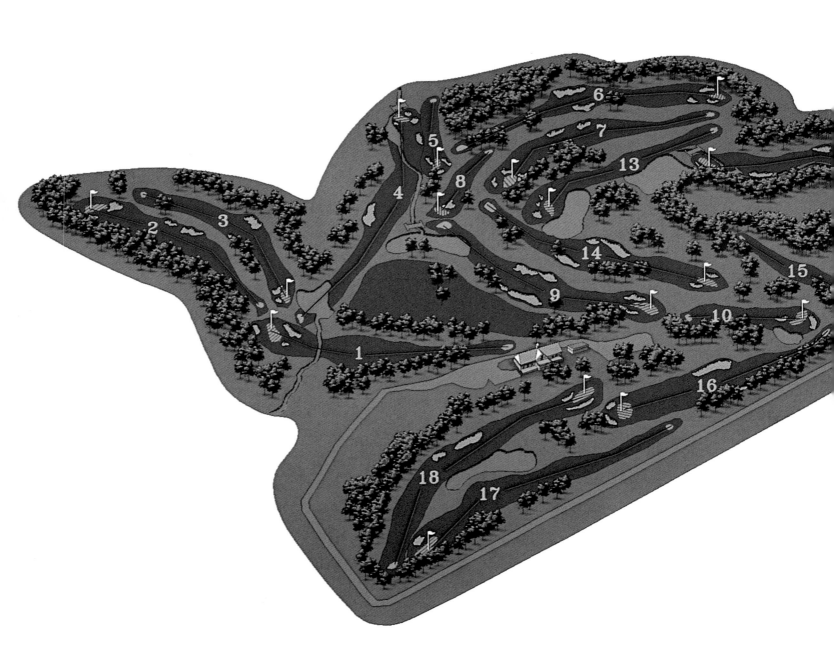

The par-three 10th marks the beginning of some of Canada's most challenging golf holes.

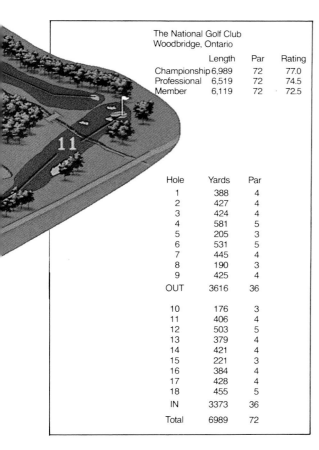

The National Golf Club Woodbridge, Ontario			
	Length	Par	Rating
Championship	6,989	72	77.0
Professional	6,519	72	74.5
Member	6,119	72	72.5

Hole	Yards	Par
1	388	4
2	427	4
3	424	4
4	581	5
5	205	3
6	531	5
7	445	4
8	190	3
9	425	4
OUT	3616	36
10	176	3
11	406	4
12	503	5
13	379	4
14	421	4
15	221	3
16	384	4
17	428	4
18	455	5
IN	3373	36
Total	6989	72

overhanging willow left.

The 11th hole provides no time to gather your wits, representing what must be one of the best par-fours in Canada. Hitting a long straight drive between bunkers right, and a hillside of tangled rough on the left, leaves a short- to mid-iron over a narrow creek into a large, undulating green. Keep in mind that the greenside rough at the National is akin to that at the U.S. Open, just the way Blechman wanted it.

Don't even consider cutting the corner on the next hole, a 500-yard, double-dogleg par-five, since accomplishing that near-impossible feat would involve carrying a stand of towering pine trees. Respect this as a true three-shot hole, laying up on your second effort. The river describes the left boundary of this beauty until it slashes across the fairway just in front of the sinister, multi-leveled green. A par on this hole is a badge of honor to be displayed with pride once back in the safe confines of the clubhouse.

Number 13 provides no respite: a 360-yard par-four that requires a drive to avoid a lake and creek on the left and ruggedly inclined rough on the right. The second shot on the dogleg-left requires a short iron to a small, well-bunkered green perched beside another pond.

No mention of The National would be complete without description of the greens. Slick, treacherous, subtle, undulating: words can scarcely hint at the work that is left once the ball reaches the putting surface. The 16th hole, perhaps one of the least remarkable in terms of design, attains mythical stature within the golfing brotherhood on the merits of its green alone. Being above the hole could mean chipping back onto the green with your next shot.

The view from the highly elevated 18th tee at The National provides seldom-equalled scenic serenity. Standing in a chute formed by tall, straight pines, you survey a good portion of the course. A clear lake on the right provides a sense of tranquil beauty but, as is The National's mischievious wont, also taunts the player to cut off as much water as he dares on his tee shot on the 445-yard uphill par-five. Overly cautious hitters will find themselves in bunkers left, blocked from the green by weeping willows. The approach shot must be high and soft to ensure the ball doesn't skid over the green into what can only be characterized as wildlife habitat.

And so it goes. The unforgiving, unforgettable National demands respect. Intelligent shot selection and a smooth swing will permit not only survival, but enjoyment.

Playing The National may not be the only way to see the course. Director of Golf Ben Kern says there are viewing areas on the course for up to 50,000 spectators and the membership is receptive to hosting the right event. "The Canadian Open, of course, the World Cup or some other significant international event would be appropriate," says the former PGA Tour player. "We have a great course and a great event would certainly showcase what we have hidden here."

Thought by many to be the toughest hole on the course, the par-four 11th rewards only two perfect shots.

Small, fast and well-protected greens are par for the National.

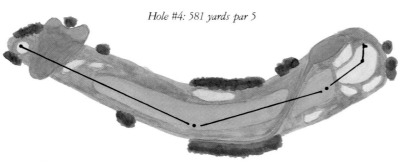

Hole #4: 581 yards par 5

Most Difficult Hole

Number 4 (581 yards, par-five) A tight, twisting double dogleg that severely punishes an errant tee shot. A meandering creek bordering dense rough lurks on the right while enormous bunkers and overhanging willow trees defend the left. The creek winds across the fairway at the 150-yard mark and continues down the left side, threatening a wayward second shot. A long but narrow green is encircled by expansive bunkers, enticing the player to lay up short of the green and offer a birdie opportunity as a reward to a precise wedge.

A traditionalist's dream, Rosedale is a refuge in the heart of Canada's largest city.

ROSEDALE
Golf Club

Architect: Donald Ross
Head Professional: John Porter
Manager: Michael Geluch
Superintendent: William Fach

Every day, tens of thousands of harried commuters inch along through the bumper-to-bumper traffic lining Ontario's major artery, Highway 401. Down the Yonge Street off-ramp they come like lemmings, heading for downtown offices. Few realize they are just a par-five away from one of Canada's oldest and greatest golf clubs—Rosedale.

Rosedale Golf Club evolved from the defunct Deer Park Club and its nine-hole layout in the late 19th Century. A publication of the time describes the club's humble beginnings: "The course was primitive in nature, the property was rented and the club was developed in a co-operative fashion when the sport held no interest for the public." But golf apparently caught the public's attention shortly thereafter, as this report from The Globe of November 28, 1896, indicates: "The fascinating game of golf is gaining steadily in popularity with the citizens of Toronto, as elsewhere, and members are still being added to the Rosedale club's list. There are now some 80 gentlemen and 60 ladies in the club, and nearly all of them may be called enthusiastic votaries of the royal game."

But the same article, titled Rosedale Golf Club, allows that golf fever was not exactly sweeping the nation. "It is not easy for spectators who know nothing about golf to understand what charm there can be in hitting a small white ball round a two- or three-mile course, and a contemptuous smile is most frequently vouchsafed by athletic visitors to the lacrosse grounds as they pass groups of able-bodied men on the putting green striving with solemn earnestness to knock the small white sphere into a little hole in the ground." The writer added that "the Rosedale course consists of 18 holes and is laid out with some ingenuity on comparatively limited grounds."

The present course, cradled in a verdant valley protected by century-old trees and nurtured by the meandering Don River, is hospitable, making up in shot values what it lacks in length. The original Donald Ross design has been touched over the years by a number of architects; the noted U.S. designer Bob Cupp was commissioned in 1988 to restore the lustre to Rosedale, a task he has performed admirably.

"This course hosted many championships

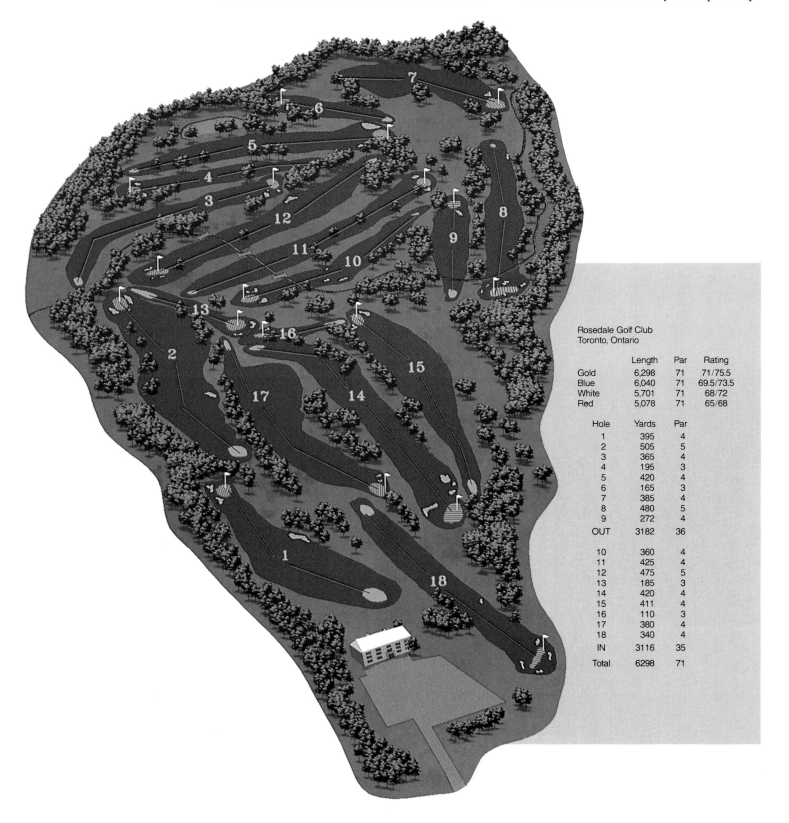

Rosedale Golf Club
Toronto, Ontario

	Length	Par	Rating
Gold	6,298	71	71/75.5
Blue	6,040	71	69.5/73.5
White	5,701	71	68/72
Red	5,078	71	65/68

Hole	Yards	Par
1	395	4
2	505	5
3	365	4
4	195	3
5	420	4
6	165	3
7	385	4
8	480	5
9	272	4
OUT	3182	36
10	360	4
11	425	4
12	475	5
13	185	3
14	420	4
15	411	4
16	110	3
17	380	4
18	340	4
IN	3116	35
Total	6298	71

in the '30s and '40s and was considered one of the top 10 in Canada in the '60s, but it has not been treated the best throughout its history," admits Head Professional John Porter. "That has changed since Cupp's involvement. That started as remodelling the bunkers, returning more to the Donald Ross style. But it became a comprehensive remodelling. When you leave the first tee at Rosedale and head down into the valley, you would swear you're not in the city. Somehow you feel safe and comfortable.

"The golf course plays longer than the card says, and positioning is vital. It's a thinking man's course. I would say that the stretch from eight through 13 is kind of our Amen Corner," says Porter, referring to the treacherous grouping of holes at Augusta National, home of the Masters tournament. "Scoring well on them is vital if you're going to have a good round. But I have to say that, thanks in part to Bob Cupp, there's not a weak hole on this golf course."

The eighth hole is a 473-yard par-five from the back tees which features the river cutting in front of the tee and then proceeding to describe the left boundary of the fairway. Three bunkers and extensive mounding around the green make for a difficult approach. The par-four ninth, while it may appear a weak sister

on the scorecard at only 272 yards from the gold tees, can just as easily result in a bogey as a birdie. Only the very confident or foolhardy would attempt to drive this tiny green, guarded by cavernous bunkers and mounds. Leave the driver in the bag on the 10th hole as well, because the river loops across the fairway at about the 220-yard mark. Number 11 is a better driving hole, 390 yards straightaway from an elevated tee. The par-five 12th is 485 yards long, with a fairway bisected by the river about 260 yards from the tee. The new two-tiered green, in its natural amphitheatre-like setting, is protected by extensive mounding and bunkers. The final hole of this challenging group is an uphill, 185-yard par-three playing into the teeth of a wind that swirls unpredictably around Rosedale's tranquil valley.

Rosedale Golf Club has been on this secluded 136-acre site in Toronto since 1910, although the club dates back to 1893, and shifted locations several times prior to putting down permanent roots. Aside from becoming one of the most respected and traditional clubs in the country, the course was good enough to host a wide spectrum of events in years gone by: Canadian Opens in 1912 and 1928, the 1924 Canadian Amateur, the Canadian Ladies' Championship in 1912, two Canadian PGA Championships, plus a variety of provincial

George S. Lyon

George S. Lyon may be the most remarkable story in golf, anywhere. Although he was a well-rounded athlete who excelled in baseball, tennis and track events, his first love was cricket. In fact, it was while Lyon was playing cricket at the Rosedale club in Toronto that he first saw golf being played; sportsman that he was, he had to try this novel activity. He was 38 years old. Within a year, he was Rosedale's leading golfer. Two years later, using what many observers criticized as a cricket swing crudely adapted to hit a golf ball, he won the first of eight Canadian Amateurs he would claim between 1898 and 1914. To that trove, he would add 10 Canadian Senior championships (the last when he was 72) and three North American Seniors titles. But Lyon's most lingering claim to fame came when he defeated a stellar field in the 1904 Olympics in St. Louis, Missouri, to win the last gold medal awarded for golf. Though 46 years old, he accepted the trophy and medal after walking the length of the room to the podium — on his hands. No wonder George S. Lyon remains known as "the grand old man of Canadian golf!"

Nestled in a river valley, Rosedale offers a rewarding experience for golfers of all abilities.

The 185-yard 13th hole is touted as one of the country's best.

competitions.

Rosedale has been largely out of the spotlight in recent years, perhaps due as much to its membership's desire to shun attention as to the inappropriateness of the course for top-level competition. With the redesign complete, perhaps it is time to resurrect these words from the official program of the 1928 Canadian Open and welcome back stately Rosedale to the upper echelon of Canadian golf: "The course of the Rosedale Golf Club is a perfect spot for a championship. It is within 40 minutes of the heart of the city by streetcar. The rolling character of the course provides many points of vantage from which spectators can follow the play. It has a commodious clubhouse and a staff capable of meeting any emergency thrust upon it."

———— Toronto, Ontario ————

ST. GEORGE'S

Golf and Country Club

Architect: *Stanley Thompson*
Head Professional: *Neil Verwey*
Manager: *Patricia Mann*
Superintendent: *John Gall*

The seclusion of St. George's Golf and Country Club, an oasis
of calm tucked out of sight near one of Toronto busiest thoroughfares,
represents in many ways the sum of all that is wonderful about
golf. Ironically, St. George's owes its beginnings to Toronto's bustling
atmosphere: it was originally opened to provide recreation for guests
at the city's then-remarkable Royal York Hotel. The course was
called the Royal York Golf Club from its inception in 1928 until
1946, when its financial arrangement ended with the Canadian Pacific
Railway, owners of the hotel.

Astutely, the founders invited Stanley Thompson of Toronto,
recognized as one of the premier course architects in the world
at the time, to design 18 holes on the convoluted, heavily treed
acreage. Thompson fulfilled his mandate admirably, producing a
layout that has stood the test of time as very few other courses
have. Head Professional Neil Verwey cites one of Thompson's
commandments when he says, "The golf course fits the terrain.
It doesn't have that 'manufactured' feel to it that a lot of new
ones do.

"Each hole is unique unto itself," says Verwey. "There is no
sameness to any of the holes at St. George's. The course is very

Stanley Thompson's classic layout has stood the test of time.

playable. The landing areas aren't tight, but you have to be very careful with your second shots and by no means are you finished once you get to the green. The par-threes here are fantastic and, of course, it has Thompson's thumbprint, which is his great fairway bunkers."

Four Canadian Opens were played on Thompson's classic layout: 1933 (won by Joe Kirkwood), 1949 (E.J. Harrison), 1960 (Art Wall) and 1968 (Bob Charles). In addition, St. George's has been a favored site for the du Maurier Ltd. Classic, designated as one of the four "major" events on the Ladies' Professional Golf Association Tour. Two-time winner JoAnne Carner (1975, 1978) says it is "the best club I have ever played; no four finer finishing holes in the world." After her second win, she commented that the final round was "the

St. George's Golf and Country Club
Toronto, Ontario

	Length	Par	Rating
Blue	6797	71	73
White	6477	71	71
Red	6205	71	69.5

Hole	Yards	Par			
1	378	4	10	377	4
2	420	4	11	517	5
3	201	3	12	383	4
4	480	5	13	214	3
5	403	4	14	446	4
6	146	3	15	580	5
7	442	4	16	203	3
8	217	3	17	447	4
9	543	5	18	400	4
OUT	3230	35	IN	3567	36
			Total	6797	71

greatest round I ever played on the toughest course I ever played." In total, St. George's played host to five du Maurier Ltd. Classics between 1975 and 1984.

Playing the course like the LPGA stars would be too much to ask, but here are a few notes from the hole-by-hole commentary prepared for the event: "The first hole is one of the finer opening holes in golf. From an elevated tee, the golfer plays to a roomy but sloping fairway. The second shot will be about 130 yards to a slightly elevated green. The prevailing wind quarters left to right. The second hole is one of the tougher holes because of the undulating terrain. The tee shot is from one elevation to another and the fairway slopes to the right. The approach will be about 180 yards to a green protected by a boundary on the left and bunkers right. The green is long and narrow, demanding precision and control from the two-iron to five-wood second shot. The third is another elevated tee shot, but the big problem here is the narrow and severely sloping green. Though the shot will be something like a three-iron, the green won't be too difficult to hit, sitting as it does so receptively below the player. But once on the green, the player will have to take care."

The finishing holes have claimed their share of competitors, the hole-by-hole commentary notes in its description of the 14th. "By now, the hills may be taking their toll on players, but anyone who can hang in there will be in good shape. Pars are the thing on these holes in the middle of the back side. Golfers will likely flirt with the left side of the fairway,

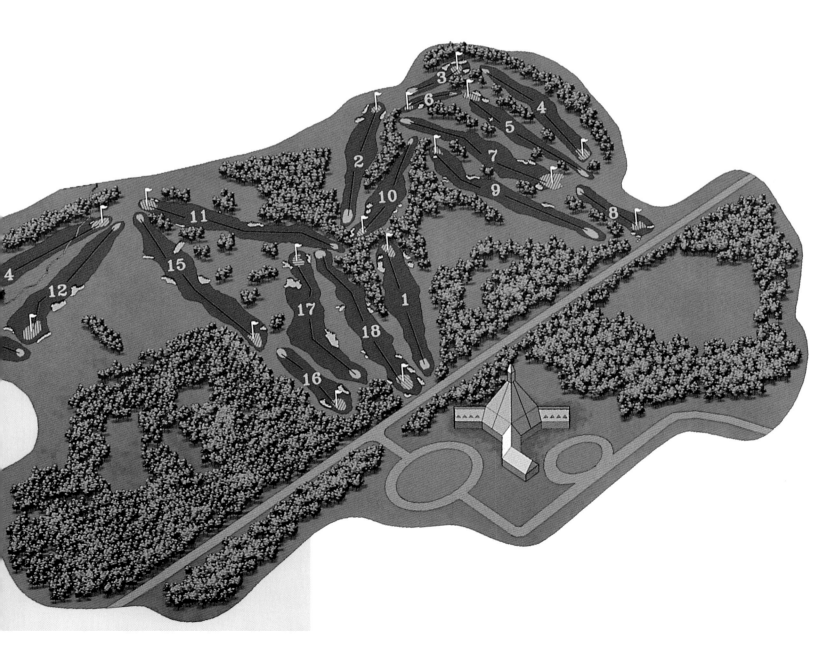

St. George's features excellent par-fours. On the 446-yard 14th, the second shot must clear the creek.

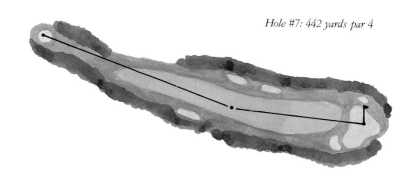

Hole #7: 442 yards par 4

The Toughest Hole at St. George's

The Number 1-rated stroke hole at St. George's Golf and Country Club is the par-four seventh hole which plays 442 yards from the blue tees and 20 yards less from the whites. Head Pro Neil Verwey respectfully suggests that you "grunt" on your tee shot. "You've got to hit the ball as far and straight as you can. Even then, you'll still be facing a long-iron or fairway wood into a very severe green. There are fairway traps and mounds all the way up the left side, and trees on both sides — and it's all uphill. Your second shot has to carry bunkers in front of the green. A super hole."

but this is the blind side from the tee. Still, those who succeed in placing their ball will have a shorter club for the second shot. It is a give-and-take hole, for the second shot from the left side will contend with a green banked on the right by a hill, and directly in line with the player's approach. The 15th is some kind of hole! After two shots down a fairway reminiscent of the first, the golfer is left with a shot up to the clouds. The green is so raised that it seems the shot is a pop fly, but it is a very difficult green to work with, angling on the front and back right.

"What a challenge these final holes are," the commentary continues. "The 16th hole takes the golfer to the perimeter of the course, not far from where she began, and offers the first of a variety of testing shots down the last stretch. Here is a green with a narrow entrance, a deep bunker right and trees left. A high fade is the shot, but that's a bit of a challenge with a long-iron. Number 17 is a slight dogleg-right where the long hitter does

have an advantage: she can try to shave yards by cutting the corner. That will leave a four- or five-iron to a well-trapped green cut on an angle. To the right is a gully and a bunker demanding a shot from eight feet down.

"Nothing like a finishing hole that leads toward a rambling old clubhouse in the distance," the summary concludes. "Victory may seem within grasp, but the approach is fraught with problems. A bunker at the left front and another at the right corner make the second shot hard on the nerves. Even if the bunkers are avoided, there is always the chance of the next being played from the sidehill lie in rough that fringes the green and bunkers. As usual, the green will be quick, and so this final hole will epitomize all that is best about St. George's as a site for a major championship: it demands the full shot mixed with the delicate touch, the knowledge to hit a variety of shots, and the good sense to know when to apply that knowledge. It demands restraint, finesse and strength."

Many championships have been decided on the 18th green: four Canadian Opens and five du Maurier Ltd. Classics among them.

— Scarborough, Ontario —

SCARBORO

Golf and Country Club

Architect: A.W. Tillinghast
Head Professional: Arthur Ewing
Manager: Tibor Veghely
Superintendent: Dennis Pellrene

When the founders of Scarboro Golf and Country Club asked George Cumming, head professional at the Toronto Golf Club, to lay out 18 holes in what was then a remote area 20 kilometres northeast of Toronto, Cumming was not unfamiliar with the property. In fact, he had inspected it previously when his club was pondering its relocation and had turned it down for various reasons. As a designer, he admired its potential and the way nature had suited it to the task at hand. Cumming noted that the acreage was a combination of "pasture, hills, gullies and forest, along a narrow, shallow creek." Its topography was ideal for a golf course, he said, and required little in the way of artificial hazards.

Little did Cumming or anyone else at that time realize that the hazards encountered by the Scarboro Golf and Country Club since its founding in 1912 would be almost entirely man-made. Its resilience and resourcefulness were tested by, among other things, two world wars (and the resulting gas rationing that isolated the membership even further), the Depression and a financial scandal that almost closed the club in the 1940s. Perhaps the most devastating obstacle encountered was the spectre of recurring floods, an act of God that periodically crippled the course for decades. That "narrow, shallow creek" that Cumming admired had an alter ego: a raging torrent that appeared after every downpour. It would rampage through the course, tearing out bridges and devouring portions of the holes which bordered it. Not for almost 80 years would the problem be resolved, through lengthy legal battles with the municipality as well as with engineering skill.

The sprawling Victorian clubhouse, with its graceful verandah, has been a Scarboro trademark since its construction in 1914. The 18th green can be seen from it, but, more importantly, it has a bird's-eye view of the 19th hole, a true 19th hole, added when "Tillie the Terror" — A.W. Tillinghast — redesigned the course in 1926. The fiendishly sloped green of this 128-yard par-three has been the cause of tens of thousands of dollars changing hands.

Tillinghast was brought in to redesign Scarboro in the wake of widespread criticism about the layout and its condition. The extremely talented designer of famed courses such as Baltusrol and Winged Foot in the United States modernized the course, lengthening it to 6,400 yards, adding bunkers and replacing greens and tees. To this day, he is acknowledged as the true architect of the course, although Stanley Thompson dabbled with the layout on a number of occasions and Cumming did the original routing. Tillinghast was a foppish eccentric and his ideas were not unanimously

admired at Scarboro, a problem that may have had to do with his working technique. Geoffrey Cornish and Ronald Whitten, in their book, The Golf Course, recount Tillie's approach: "During course construction, he would routinely appear in his three-piece suit, plant a shooting stick in the shade, settle his bulk on it, sip from a flask and shout directions all day long to the laborers."

Bud Donovan, Scarboro's amateur historian, is quoted in Louis Cauz's exhaustive unpublished history of the club: "Tillinghast had the foresight to preserve the natural beauty of the course and built one that you can either pitch your ball onto the green or pitch-and-run it on. You can do this on all but the 11th and 15th. There aren't many courses like that today. The creek is a natural source of trouble as you have to go over it 11 times and, on six holes, you have the creek running adjacent to the fairway. It's an old-fashioned course."

The course has played host to a wide range of amateur and professional tournaments over the years, including Canadian Opens in 1940 (won by Sam Snead), 1947 (Bobby Locke), 1953 (Dave Douglas) and 1963 (Doug Ford). One of the more unusual events was the 1961 World Series of Golf, pitting the previous year's Masters champion (Arnold Palmer) against the winner of the British Open (Gary Player). Player downed Palmer 67-69. The 1958 Canadian Amateur here saw Scarboro member Eric

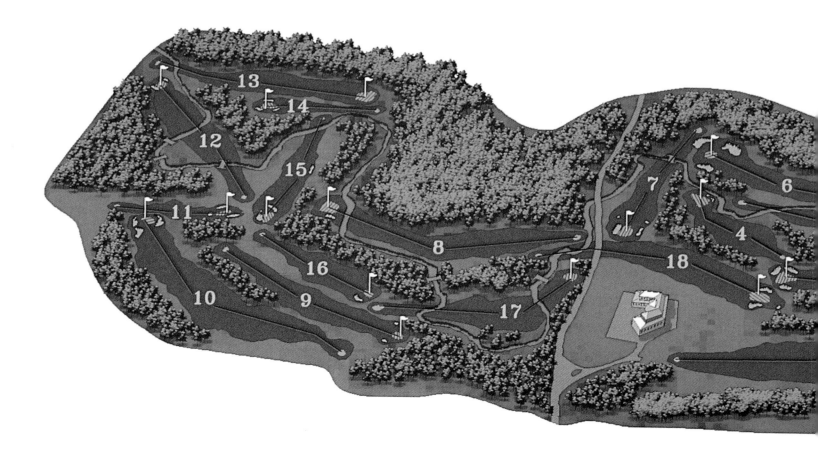

Hanson lose one-up to Bruce Castator of Weston Golf and Country Club.

One of Scarboro's most accomplished players was the fabled Donald Day Carrick. He won the 1923 Ontario Junior at the age of 16, and won his second U.S. Junior the following year. By his 21st birthday, he had notched two Canadian Amateur victories and was hailed as "the Bobby Jones of Canada." Made an honorary member of the club at the age of 18, Carrick disappointed many when he sidestepped golf and became a national boxing champion, competing for Canada as an Olympic light-heavyweight. The multi-faceted Carrick went on to become a Harvard- and Osgoode-educated lawyer. When he made a brief golfing comeback in the 1930s, he managed to win the Ontario Amateur and set a Scarboro course record of 63 that stood for 50 years.

Carrick, then 81, is quoted in Cauz's 1987 book: "Scarboro was the place to learn to play golf. You had to hit the ball straight or you would be penalized, and you had to be exacting

Scarboro Golf and Country Club Scarborough, Ontario			Length	Par	Rating
		Blue	6376	71	71
		White	6047	71	69.5
		Yellow	5666	73	72.5
		Red	5369	73	71

Hole	Yards	Par			
			10	527	5
1	576	5	11	110	3
2	213	3	12	416	4
3	342	4	13	417	4
4	205	3	14	212	3
5	439	4	15	285	4
6	526	5	16	284	4
7	276	4	17	379	4
8	413	4	18	377	4
9	380	4	IN	3007	35
OUT	3369	36	Total	6376	71

with your drives. I rarely used my driver. But it was a fun place to play, with the creek wandering through it the way it did. It also had excellent greens."

Another great player — often called "the greatest Canadian amateur never to win the Canadian Amateur" — was Phil Farley, three-time runner-up in the national amateur championship. His record was astounding: six Ontario Amateurs, two Ontario Opens, two Quebec Opens, seven-time low amateur in the Canadian Open, 16 Willingdon Cup teams, a Commonwealth team member, and much more. He served as president of both the Ontario Golf Association and the Royal Canadian Golf Association. His contribution to Canadian golf is commemorated by the "Phil Farley Memorial Trophy for the Senior Interprovincial Team Matches," conducted by the RCGA.

While Carrick and Farley dominate the amateur side of Scarboro, it is the larger-than-life portrait of former head professional Bob Gray that stands head-and-shoulders above the rest. As Louis Cauz writes: "Instead of listing the number of years he won the Rivermead Cup for the lowest 72-hole score by a home-brew in the Canadian Open, his Ontario and Quebec Open titles, his Millar Trophy triumphs in match play among Canadian pros, his course records, or the year he was runner-up by two measly strokes to Sam Snead in the Canadian Open with a 276 (a score good enough to win 49 other Opens), let's enjoy the anecdotes that earned Bobby Gray the accolade as the most lovable character to ever man a pro shop or act as a golf course maitre d' in Canada." The list of anecdotes in Cauz's book goes on for page after page: a fitting tribute to the man who personified Scarboro from 1937 until his death in 1966.

If you're wondering why the club is "Scarboro" and the municipality "Scarborough," so is everyone else. Apparently, there is no logical explanation. Tillinghast would have been proud.

The 10th hole at Scarboro — a product of the eccentric genius of A.W. Tillinghast.

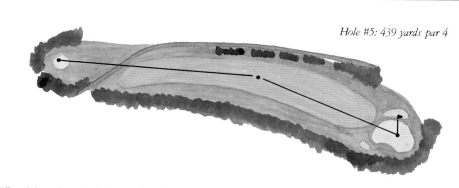

Hole #5: 439 yards par 4

The Toughest Hole at Scarboro

The fifth hole at Scarboro Golf and Country Club plays to 439 yards from the blue tees and 427 from the whites. Outstanding Canadian amateur Nick Weslock has called it "one of the great holes on the continent." This par-four is one of the many holes on which the creek comes into play. In this case, the river cuts diagonally across the fairway, out about 175 yards on the right to about 200 yards on the left, before continuing down the left side of the fairway. Hitting the driver long and straight is the key.

Most greens at Scarboro, like the fifth pictured here, are accessible along the ground or through the air.

—— Richmond Hill, Ontario ——

SUMMIT

Golf and Country Club

Architects: *George Cumming, Stanley Thompson*
Head Professional: *Ron Rayner*
Manager: *Marinus Gerritsen*
Superintendent: *Scott Dodson*

Appropriately, the word "summit" is synonymous with "pinnacle" or "ultimate." In the case of the Summit Golf and Country Club, such a label is not really an overstatement on several counts. Not only does the course sit on some of the highest ground in the region, it has one of the top golfing records of any Canadian club and is one of the finest layouts in the country.

Although founded in 1912 in the wooded hills some 35 kilometres north of the heart of Toronto, this superb course had a troubled early history due in part to its then-remote location and financial difficulties encountered as a result of the First World War. The original layout was done in 1912 by George Cumming, the head professional at the Toronto Golf Club. Cumming was eminently qualified. He arrived at Toronto in 1900 from Scotland to work at the Toronto club and in the years since had won the Canadian Open in 1905 and finished second three times.

Cumming had the assistance of another accomplished golfer, George S. Lyon, who has become a Canadian golf legend for his domination of the Canadian Amateur in the early years of this century and for winning the gold medal in golf at the 1904 Olympics in St. Louis. Upon arriving at the secluded Summit property,

Cumming and Lyon discovered rolling acres of sandy loam — the ideal base for a course — covered with robust trees ranging from maples to black walnuts. Their routing took full advantage of the region's natural contours, starting with the elevated first tee and concluding with the 18th green that sits on a plateau under the present clubhouse veranda.

Despite their anticipation, the course they had charted laid dormant until 1919 when it was substantially altered by Stanley Thompson of Toronto, one of the premier architects in North America at the time. The Cumming-Lyon layout was opened semi-officially in that same year, with temporary tees and greens, amid much hullabaloo. The war had ended and everyone wanted to erase the memory of those grim years. By 1921, Thompson's revisions

were effected and finally, a tribute to perseverance and love of the game, Summit Golf and Country Club opened officially for play once and for all. Thanks to a dedicated core of only 48 members during the Second World War, the club again staved off financial ruin. These volunteers cut the fairways with hay mowers and tees and greens with lawnmowers. Their efforts paid off: by 1949, Summit's membership roll included 375 names in all categories.

Despite the many changes to the course, by Bob Cupp and Doug Carrick among others, playing Summit reveals that it remains true to Thompson's fundamentals, outlined in a booklet called About Golf Courses: Their Construction and Upkeep. "Nature must always be the architect's model," he wrote. "The

The fourth hole is one of the very few times water is in play at Summit.

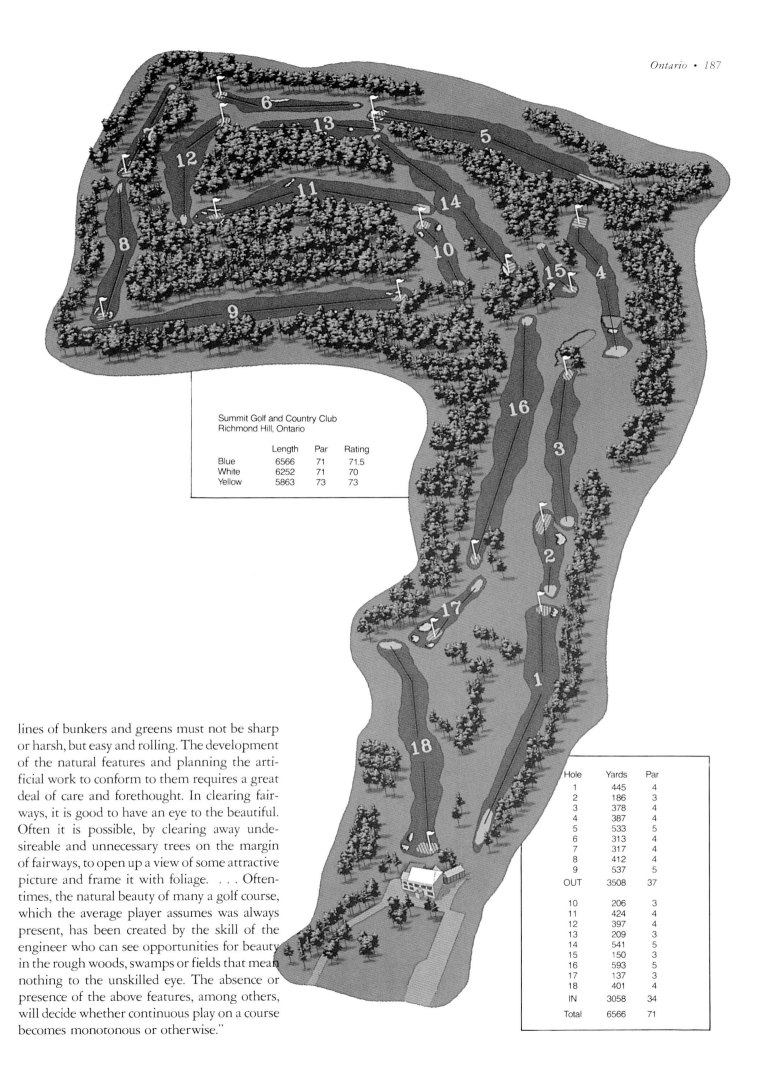

Summit Golf and Country Club
Richmond Hill, Ontario

	Length	Par	Rating
Blue	6566	71	71.5
White	6252	71	70
Yellow	5863	73	73

lines of bunkers and greens must not be sharp or harsh, but easy and rolling. The development of the natural features and planning the artificial work to conform to them requires a great deal of care and forethought. In clearing fairways, it is good to have an eye to the beautiful. Often it is possible, by clearing away undesireable and unnecessary trees on the margin of fairways, to open up a view of some attractive picture and frame it with foliage. . . . Oftentimes, the natural beauty of many a golf course, which the average player assumes was always present, has been created by the skill of the engineer who can see opportunities for beauty in the rough woods, swamps or fields that mean nothing to the unskilled eye. The absence or presence of the above features, among others, will decide whether continuous play on a course becomes monotonous or otherwise."

Hole	Yards	Par
1	445	4
2	186	3
3	378	4
4	387	4
5	533	5
6	313	4
7	317	4
8	412	4
9	537	5
OUT	3508	37
10	206	3
11	424	4
12	397	4
13	209	3
14	541	5
15	150	3
16	593	5
17	137	3
18	401	4
IN	3058	34
Total	6566	71

The par-three 17th hole requires a delicate shot, avoiding the sentinel tree.

Judging from the number of longtime members at Summit and the reviews from topnotch players who have participated in tournaments here, Thompson achieved his goal in glorious fashion. In addition, the course has become a drawing card for internationally renowned architects from Pete Dye to Jack Nicklaus, who admire its timeless excellence without exception.

Just two years after its opening, Summit played host to the Canadian PGA Championship, won by Percy Barrett, the head pro at the Lambton club in Toronto. Barrett collected $150 of the total $450 purse, not a bad take, considering upper- middle-class houses in the city were selling for less than $10,000. The course was also the site of the 1987 Canadian Seniors tournament, won by Moe Norman. In the intervening years, Summit's 18 challenging and often underrated holes saw competition in dozens of regional, provincial and national championships between men, women, juniors and seniors.

"Summit is a tournament course because it demands what all tournament courses demand: ball control, reasonable length, a sharp short game and deft putting," says Lorne Rubenstein, author of Summit's club history. "The greens are well enough placed, with enough pin positions, that a golfer who hopes to score the course must be able to hit his ball to the right locations. And when the greens are quick, their slope is enough to touch on any competitor's nervous tendencies."

Former Summit head professional Ken Girard is quoted in Rubenstein's book as saying: "To score well at Summit, a player must have down pat the short pitch shot and the high cut shot. At Summit, 14 of 18 greens are in some degree of elevation, which require many types of wedge shots. The greens are rolling, reasonably small and well bunkered."

Summit's Toughest Hole

Summit's Number 1 handicap hole is the par-four 11th. Called "Blind," it plays to 424 yards from the back tees and 414 from the whites. This hole has been the centre of controversy almost since the day the course opened. In 1925, the greens committee said the members felt a hole that doglegged to the left but had a fairway that sloped right was unfair. Compounding this inequity were mounds that undulated into the landing area, obscuring the hole from the tee, and a cavernous waste bunker on the right.

Despite those early and ongoing objections, the same obstacles are present today. To avoid disaster, hit your drive as tight to the left as possible — seemingly a contradiction on a dogleg-left. Console yourself with the fact that the bend is slight and you will be hitting a mid-iron to one of the larger greens on the course. Factor into your club selection the fact that the green slopes from back to front, like many of Summit's putting surfaces, so don't be above the hole.

Summit is the epitome of a mature, traditional parkland course.

Toronto Golf Club is a classic H.S. Colt masterpiece that has remained almost unchanged since 1912.

TORONTO

Golf Club

Architect: Harry Colt
Head Professional: Doug Rankin
Manager: Glenn Smale
Superintendent: Robert Brewster

The Toronto Golf Club is the third-oldest golf club in Canada and, not surprisingly, steeped in tradition. One of its many celebrity guests, comedian Danny Kaye, recognized this with the quip: "The club is so traditional that I kept wondering when somebody was going to turn on the gas lights."

Founded in 1876, this club is quite content with — indeed, proud of — its roots, which are entwined with those of the family trees of Toronto's gentry. Perusing membership rolls and lists of past presidents and club captains provides a glimpse of Toronto's history-makers: Osler, Seagram, Cockshutt, Cassels, and many more. The club champions' list includes Hall of Famer George S. Lyon, gold medalist in golf at the 1904 Olympics. Toronto also produced many other fine players in its early days such as 1897 Canadian Amateur champion Archie Kerr and the great Andy Smith.

And, not so very long ago, the club manager at the time, Fred Armitage, resisted instituting the modern method of members' numbers when signing for food and drink. Armitage, known as "Mr. Secretary," could identify every member's handwriting. As final evidence of this respect for tradition, Toronto Golf has had but five professionals in almost a century, with the incumbent, Doug

Rankin, taking over in 1991 from John Hunt, who served from 1959. Arthur Smith was employed for only four years, 1895-99, while the esteemed George Cumming occupied the post with great distinction for the next half-century. His son, Lou, was head professional for the subsequent nine years until his untimely death.

The tradition dates back to 1870 when a Scotsman named Farquharson Smith travelled from Quebec City to visit his brother James Lamond Smith, a Toronto banker. For whatever reason — being a Scotsman was probably enough — Farquharson packed along a few balls and his golf clubs. Another factor in his decision could be that he was an avid golfer, and would be involved in what would become the Royal Quebec Golf Club in 1874. In any case, the clubs and balls were put to good use by the brothers and their acquaintances at Lamond's summer home in what now is the east end of Toronto.

Although Farquharson returned to Quebec City, he had infected that small band of aficionados with golfing fever. The club's history notes that Colonel G.A. Sweny, who eventually joined them, summed up public reaction to the new craze succinctly: "It is needless to say that they were treated with a contemptuous but pitiful regard." Pitiful though they may have been, they formed a club in 1876, naming Lamond Smith its first captain and laying out nine crude holes near his summer retreat. It was the first golf club in North America west of Montreal, but was joined quickly by pioneers in other Ontario centres such as Brantford, Niagara-on-the-Lake, Hamilton and Kingston.

Inter-club matches soon were underway and Toronto would play host to numerous regional, provincial and national tournaments throughout its history. Canadian Opens in 1905 (won by host professional George Cumming), 1909 (Karl Keffer of Royal Ottawa), 1914 (Keffer),

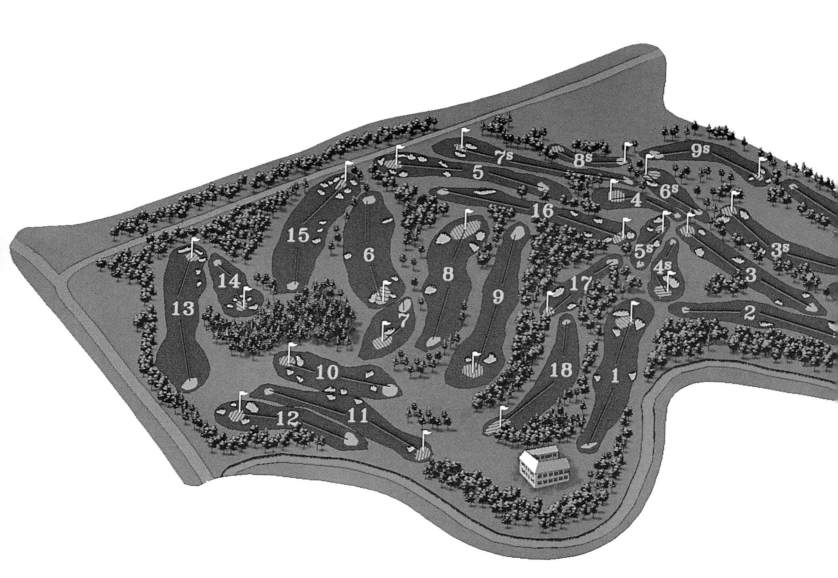

Toronto Golf Club's peaceful beauty sits in contrast to reminders of the city's industry.

Hole	Yards	Par
1	357	4
2	384	4
3	443	4
4	187	3
5	460	4
6	387	4
7	180	3
8	400	4
9	451	4
OUT	3249	34
10	330	4
11	391	4
12	364	4
13	515	5
14	148	3
15	391	4
16	492	5
17	218	3
18	339	4
IN	3188	36
Total	6437	70

Toronto Golf Club
Port Credit, Ontario

	Length	Par	Rating
Championship	6437	70	71
Red	6185	70	70
Yellow	6020	75	75

Superb conditioning and unobtrusive hazards make Toronto Golf Club a true challenge.

George Cumming

The Toronto Golf Club's history, written by Jack Batten, calls George Cumming "a golfer, teacher and gentleman of the old school, which is to say a school that matches good manners with wit and kindness." That uncommon combination served Cumming well during the 50 years he served as Toronto's head professional. Golfer? Without question: Among other triumphs, he won the 1905 Canadian Open and finished second in 1906, 1907, 1909 and 1914. The last two must have rankled — champion Karl Keffer was a former assistant of Cumming's and both events took place at the Toronto Golf Club. Teacher? Keffer's success aside, thousands of pupils either learned the game or honed their abilities under his watchful eye. Gentleman of wit? An anecdote from Batten's book may suffice: A prospective female student showed up one day. "Mr. Cumming, I understand you swear," she said timorously. "Oh no," Cumming responded, with a twinkle in his eye. "I never swear. For God's sake, I'd never do such a damned thing." Born in Scotland in 1879, the short, stocky pro came to the Toronto Golf Club from his homeland in 1900, bringing little more than one of the most graceful golf swings ever seen on either side of the Atlantic. He represented all that was golf in general, and Toronto Golf Club in particular, for a half-century before passing away at his home in 1950.

1921 (W.H. Trovinger) and 1927 (Tommy Armour) were highlights of the golfing calendar until the increased pressures of parking and spectators precluded Toronto from hosting major events. The club does, however, continue to graciously invite a number of amateur events onto its genteel links.

In 1912, Toronto's membership reacted to the ominous urban sprawl by moving to new quarters in relatively remote Port Credit, near Lake Ontario. The architect was Harry Colt, the Englishman whose claim to fame was the new course at Sunningdale near London in his homeland. The new Toronto course won acclaim in its very first year, hosting the Canadian Amateur Championship and an exhibition match pitting Britain's Harry Vardon, a six-time winner of the British Open, and Ted Ray against Cumming and Percy Barrett, the professional at Toronto Lambton. Vardon and Ray won on the final hole.

Although overjoyed by the remarkable success of its men — Lyon, Kerr and Smith chief among them — Toronto could point with pride at the unequalled success of its women: Ada Mackenzie, Sydney Pepler Mulqueen, the Smith sisters (Cecil and Maude), Mrs. R.W. Gouin-lock, Mrs. Alex McBain, Mrs. E.W. Whittington, and others. This group, led by Mackenzie, dominated ladies' golf in Canada for years. It can be said without equivocation that Mackenzie, now in the Canadian Golf Hall of Fame, won every ladies' golf title of any consequence in the country.

John Hunt, the longtime head professional who retired in 1990, harks back to the theme of "tradition" when talking about the course. "We're very proud of this course, of the fact that it was designed by Harry Colt, that it is unique and that we've tried to keep it the way he intended it," Hunt says. "No changes are taken lightly here because we want to retain the character of this course. The front nine, although it is a par-34, is tough. It seems you're always hitting drives and long-irons. The back nine, par-36, is relatively easy: drives and short-irons.

"It's a wonderful golf course. The trees have grown up over the years and separate the holes so totally that it's like having 18 different golf courses. I'd call the Toronto Golf Club a comfortable, yet challenging, course. You could play here every day and enjoy it."

The 11th hole characterizes the par-36 back nine.

The 148-yard 12th hole is like most holes at Westmount: trees, rough and bunkers conspire to punish a wayward shot.

———— Kitchener-Waterloo, Ontario ————

WESTMOUNT

Golf and Country Club

Architect: Stanley Thompson
Head Professional: Rob Strahan
Manager: Terry Cowan
Superintendent: Hugh Kirkpatrick

To say that the golfing fanatics of the Kitchener-Waterloo area of Southern Ontario were desperate for golf in the early years of the 20th Century is an understatement. In 1929, when the first meetings to found the Westmount Golf and Country Club were held, there was only one course in the vicinity: Grand River Golf Club in Bridgeport, some miles distant. The golfers' resourcefulness was equalled only by their irreverence: some were seen hitting balls in the new Mount Hope Cemetery, a situation that was recorded as a "most unusual" complaint by the cemetary committee.

Those eager golfers wouldn't have long to wait. Those meetings in 1929 were dominated by Seagrams and Sniders, and these pillars of the community produced rapid action. That same year, portions of two farms were amalgamated to produce the 145 acres needed for an 18-hole layout and clubhouse. One farm belonged to Howard Snider, who would remain linked to the course for more than 30 years. He worked on the construction of Westmount and then stayed on as greens superintendent. Part of his deal for selling his farm to the club was to accept payment in the form of a lifelong annuity. The financially astute and hardy Snider lived well into his 90s after retiring in 1960.

his 90s after retiring in 1960.

The original layout, crafted by Stanley Thompson of Toronto, played over 6,440 yards with a par of 71 and remained largely untouched until additional land was obtained in 1958. At that time, the first three holes were turned into practice holes and, although the numbering has changed on the front nine, the other 15 holes — including the entire back nine — are more or less the same as they were in 1930. Again due to the dynamic leadership of the club, the course was in play by April 1931 at a total cost of less than $50,000. (New cars at the time cost $2,000, houses $3,000, and a good meal 40 cents.) A month later, the Tudor-style clubhouse, built along the lines of a 16-Century English manor, was in use and remains today. It was, by its lath-and-plaster construction, a curiosity in a region where most buildings were made of clay brick.

While the energy of the club could not be disputed, its timing was less than ideal. Canada at this time was in the grip of the Great Depression, so few improvements were made to Westmount. But when a rug was needed

"The most underrated hole" — the 407-yard 15th has been a turning point in tournaments.

for the lounge area, the members' ingenuity came to the fore. One enterprising member, Claude Musselman, arranged for a slot machine to be installed, and even in those desperate economic times, it raised an average of $125 every week. The rug was quickly paid for and the slot machine became the club's chief source of revenue. The men's fees were $60 a year and the women's $30. They would stay at that astoundingly low level for 16 years, at which time they went up by $7.50.

Westmount, described in its club history as "a challenge to the most experienced player," has certainly proven that throughout the years. The most recent event of international significance was in 1990 when the du Maurier Ltd. Classic, one of the four "majors" on the Ladies' Professional Golf Association Tour, was played here. Won by Cathy Johnston of North Carolina, the event capped an enviable tournament record. Westmount also played host to the country's best female amateurs in 1965. Ironically, the winner was Jocelyne Bourassa, who went on to star on the LPGA Tour before becoming tournament director of the du Maur-

Westmount Golf and Country Club Kitchener-Waterloo, Ontario				Hole	Yards	Par		10	337	4
				1	561	5		11	552	5
				2	375	4		12	148	3
	Length	Par	Rating	3	200	3		13	552	5
Blue	6904	73	73.5	4	422	4		14	378	4
White	6659	73	72	5	569	5		15	407	4
Red	6309	73	70.5	6	206	3		16	451	4
Gold	5738	73	68.1	7	500	5		17	165	3
				8	282	4		18	382	4
				9	417	4		IN	3372	36
				OUT	3532	37		Total	6904	73

ier Ltd. Classic. The 1981 Canadian PGA Championship, then known as the Labatt's International, attracted more than 30,000 fans, and was won by U.S. PGA Tour star Raymond Floyd. The club hosted many other events, including the 1969 Canadian Amateur (Wayne McDonald), and the 1957 Canadian Open. George Bayer won that event in a playoff over Bo Wininger. But no matter what the event, every competitor found the "challenge" that Westmount is famous for.

Head Professional Rob Strahan's first impression of Westmount was of "a grand old lady of a golf course. There appeared to be nothing tricky; that everything was laid out in front of you." While this lady may not be tricky, it has one persistent, devilish quality, he says: "There's almost no such thing as a flat lie on this course. You can hit it right down the middle and have an uphill or sidehill lie. On some holes, you don't want to be in the middle of the fairway; you want to hit to a certain area on one side or the other."

According to Strahan, the 15th and 16th holes are "game-breakers," turning points in either tournament play or a friendly match

The 200-yard third hole with its distracting pond and fountain.

among members. "Number 15 is the most underrated hole at Westmount. It's a tough, deceiving, 410-yard par-four with a green that's elevated about 40 feet. It's in one of the few open areas of the course, and the crosswind can play havoc with your shots. Take an extra club on your approach, because if you're short, you're facing a straight uphill chip and you'll have trouble just keeping your balance, much less hitting it close to the hole. I was seven-under when I got to this hole once and when I walked away, I was four-under — and I was

never off the fairway."

The 16th is another lengthy par-four and, when played in the afternoon, is straight into the setting sun and the prevailing wind. "You need the power fade here," says Strahan. "Hit a big left-to-right tee shot out at least 220 over the hill and your ball should roll down the other side. You should be hitting a four- or five-iron in here, but you're dead if you're above the hole. This green can break from six to eight feet and slopes from back to front. If you're short, you can usually get up and down."

Gary Cowan's Best Shot

The United States Amateur Championship, arguably the premier amateur tournament in the world, has been won three times by Canadians. C. Ross (Sandy) Somerville of London, Ontario, won it first in 1932 on his way to the Canadian Golf Hall of Fame. Then, in 1966, Gary Cowan of Westmount Golf and Country Club won it — but not for the last time. His playoff victory, 75-76, over favorite Deane Beman (who went on to become commissioner of the PGA Tour), capped an admirable come-from-behind effort. Five years later, Cowan found himself in a different situation: he was leading the tournament the final day. On 18, he had only to par the dogleg-left par-four to claim his second U.S. Amateur title. But his drive found the rough 135 yards from the hole. He hooded the face of his nine-iron, slashed through the ankle-deep grass, and watched as the ball headed for the flag. The shouts and screams of the gallery at first made him fear he had gone over the back of the green. Instead, the ball had trickled into the hole for an eagle two! "It was the greatest shot of my life," he told Canadian golf writer James Fitchette. For Cowan, born in Kitchener in 1938, the U.S. Amateur titles crowned a stellar career which included victories in the Canadian Amateur, the U.S. North and South Amateur, the Ontario Amateur (nine times), the New Zealand Invitational and innumerable others. In 1990, Cowan overcame tough odds and qualified for the U.S. Senior PGA Tour.

The entire back nine at Westmount remains just as Stanley Thompson designed it in 1929.

Weston is famous for its treacherous greens, such as this one on the par-four fifth hole.

WESTON

Golf and Country Club

Architect: Willie Park Jr.
Head Professional: Herb Holzscheiter
Manager: Michael Jory
Superintendent: Thom Charters

The Weston Golf and Country Club is best known as the site of Arnold Palmer's first professional victory. While Palmer's win at the 1955 Canadian Open at Weston was a memorable occasion, it is not the sole reason the course is recognized as one of Canada's best.

Weston was founded in 1914 following a town-hall meeting at which local businessmen decided to rent land in the nearby Humber Valley to construct a course. Initially, they built a crude four-hole course which served as an adventurous but adequate start. The area also served as a pasture and one of the first problems was keeping grazing cattle off the greens.

With a growing membership, the course soon expanded to nine holes and Percy Barrett, who had been an assistant to the famous Harry Vardon in Britain and runner-up in the first Canadian Open in 1904, was hired as the first professional.

Barrett was a strict disciplinarian. One day, when he was about to hit his drive off the first tee, he wheeled around and pointed his finger at a caddie. "You were talking," accused Barrett. "No sir, I was not talking," the caddie boldly replied. "Well," said the gruff Barrett, "you were going to."

In 1921, the club purchased the land it had been renting, as well as some surrounding acreage, and hired Willie Park Jr., a noted Scottish architect who twice had won the British Open, to design an 18-hole layout. The design was well-received and, with the war over, applications for membership came in droves. The fees for 1921 were set at $60 for gentlemen and $30 for ladies. In 1922, the course was opened officially with much pomp that included an exhibition match with English professionals Sandy Taylor and Alex Herd taking on Barrett and 1905 Canadian Open champion George Cumming of the Toronto Golf Club.

While the course has remained virtually unchanged from Park's admirable original design, nature has forced a few alterations. Most of those have come at the spectacular second hole, now a 314-yard par-four that has become the course's signature. Players tee off from a precipice 120 feet above a fairway bounded on the right by a pond and on the left by rough and trees. The green sits at the foot of a towering railway trestle which dominates the landscape.

In the past, however, this hole was a par-three, only to be destroyed by the flooding of the Humber River during Hurricane Hazel four decades ago. For a time, it became a lengthy par-four with a green on the far side of the trestle. The players' challenge was to decide whether to go under or over the ominous structure.

Anyone who plays Weston for the first time is struck by the immaculate conditioning, another trademark of the course. The 6,698-yard layout is kept in impeccable shape and possesses lightning-fast greens. In fact, veteran PGA Tour star Raymond Floyd has compared their speed with that at major championships such as The Masters. The greens are, for the most part, small and very deceiving. Scoring well at Weston requires patience and a smooth stroke on the greens.

Weston is a traditional course in every sense

| Weston Golf and Country Club | | | |
| Weston, Ontario | | | |

	Length	Par	Rating
Blue	6698	72	72
White	6465	72	71
Yellow	5889	74	73

Hole	Yards	Par
1	413	4
2	314	4
3	472	5
4	156	3
5	424	4
6	385	4
7	571	5
8	131	3
9	448	4
OUT	3314	36
10	337	4
11	235	3
12	471	5
13	376	4
14	438	4
15	192	3
16	541	5
17	350	4
18	444	4
IN	3384	36
Total	6698	72

of the word. The majority of holes are lined with maple, oak and spruce trees from tee to green, and a level stance on the fairways is a rare treat. The course ebbs and flows with many natural changes in elevation and scenery. There are no gimmicks at Weston; what you see is what you get.

A linkage of three holes — the fifth, sixth and seventh — provide one of the best tests of golf in Canada, and many a match has been won or lost here despite their early appearance in the round. The first two are long par-fours with danger lurking on both sides of their fairways. Both are remarkable for their extremely difficult greens that require precision placement of approach shots and careful study of the resulting putts. Ending up on the wrong side of the pin almost certainly assures a disastrous three-putt. The last in this tough trio is a tremendous 571-yard par-five with the tee set back in a tree-lined chute. To have any chance of reaching the green in two shots,

The eighth hole, although only 131 yards long, yields more bogies than birdies.

players must power a drive to the top of a knoll which cuts across the fairway. Being short of the crest can result in a blind second shot, the outcome being a bogey, or worse.

Weston's 18th hole presents a challenging completion to a round. A 444-yard par-four, the downhill dogleg-left plays shorter than its yardage indicates, but requires a brilliant tee shot. The green rarely holds anything but a superb approach and a bump-and-run strategy is often best. Once there, heed the members' credo that all putts break to the clubhouse, although you'll be hard pressed to do so since your eyes tend to deceive you on this subtle putting surface.

Weston has an impressive tournament history. In addition to the 1955 Canadian Open, it has played host to the 1971 Ontario Open, won by the late George Knudson, and Ontario Amateurs in 1964 and 1978, both won by Gary Cowan. In 1990, to honor its 75th anniversary, the club opened its doors to the Cadillac Classic skins game, featuring Palmer, Floyd, Mark Calcavecchia and eventual winner Dave Barr of Richmond, B.C. The year was capped by the hosting of the Canadian Amateur championship, won, fittingly, by Weston member Warren Sye.

Weston is perennially rated one of the best conditioned courses in Canada.

The 16th hole with its elevated green plays even longer than the 541 yards on the card.

Birth of a Legend

In 1955, a 25-year-old rookie professional named Arnold Palmer had his back to the wall. He had been shut out on the PGA Tour despite winning the U.S. Amateur the previous year and had enough money to last just six more weeks on tour. Coming to Weston Golf and Country Club to face a stellar field for the Canadian Open, he couldn't be blamed for feeling despondent. "I was frustrated with my play," Palmer recalls. "I felt I had been playing well, but I wasn't getting any results." But playing on a rain-soaked course that yielded low scores, Palmer sat in second place after the first round, firing a 64 to trail Charley Sifford by a shot. He improved on that standing the following day, shooting 67 to take the lead. The third round, he achieved another 64 in a curious manner: three shots that appeared headed for the woods caromed back into play after hitting spectators. At 21 under par after three rounds, Palmer coasted through the final day with a 70. The winner's cheque for $2,400 staked him on his way to becoming one of the best golfers of all time.

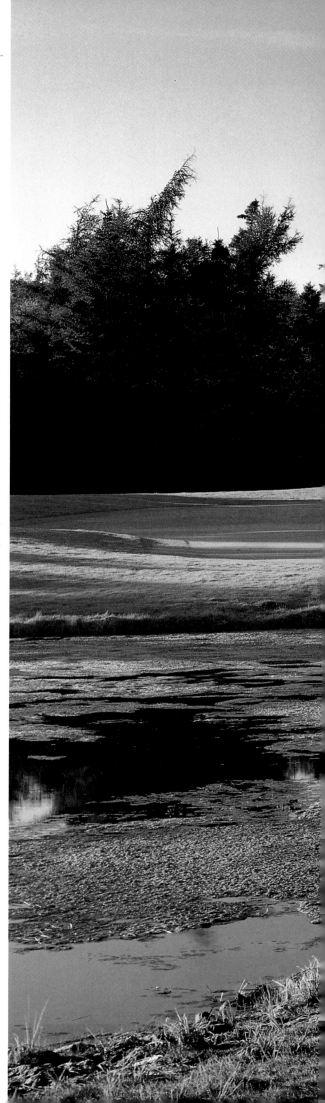

The par-five 11th hole at Brudenell River offers a birdie chance — if you clear the pond.

BRUDENELL RIVER

Provincial Golf Course

Architect: C.E. (Robbie) Robinson
Professional: Ronald Giggey
Manager: Harry Simmons
Superintendent: Dale Murchison

Prince Edward Island, a popular vacation playground with a reputation for enormous beaches and equally expansive lobster suppers, could be Canada's golfing secret. The courses range from the delightful Green Gables to the tricky Mill River, but chief among them is Brudenell River. Brudenell is much like the people of P.E.I. — uncompromising, but fair.

In 1969, the provincial government enlisted the late Canadian architect Robbie Robinson to design a golf course on what had been a 200-acre farm overlooking the Brudenell River. Robinson deftly turned the gently rolling farmland to his purposes and crafted a fine layout with a slightly different twist: the resulting course features six par-threes, six par-fours and six par-fives.

Although Brudenell River, part of a 1,400-acre provincial park complete with accommodations, sees about 35,000 golfers every season, it is seldom crowded. Harry Simmons, operations manager for Eastern P.E.I. Provincial Parks, has been involved with the golf course since it opened.

"We're slightly off the beaten track," he explains. "Also, many of our members are local farmers and fishermen whose play time is confined to between plantings and harvests, or after the catch

Brudenell River's signature hole: the par-three 10th.

at the end of the day. In fact, there are quiet times when it's possible to have the course all to yourself." This is especially true outside of peak vacation periods, but call for a tee time just in case.

After limbering up on the excellent practice range, the opening hole could offer the first of several birdie opportunities. At 404 yards from the back tees (375 from the whites), this par-four rewards a good drive down the right side with a short-iron approach to a receptive green. The putting surfaces at Brudenell River are generally quite large, a Robbie Robinson signature.

Don't make the mistake of assuming the first hole's generosity is a sign of weakness. You will be rudely awakened on the second tee, facing a 472-yard uphill par-four. "It requires a long drive and an accurate long iron or wood, depending on the wind," says Head Professional Ron Giggey. Hitting that much club into this big, rolling green with its surrounding grassy mounds will no doubt leave a challenging two-putt for par.

The aforementioned wind is what the locals call "the Brudenell Breeze." It sweeps in off the Atlantic and up the river each morning around 10 and departs without warning at 4 p.m., diabolically designed to create havoc at peak golfing hours. Keep this in mind when hitting high approach shots to tricky pin positions. Otherwise, you could encounter some of the water that comes into play on at least half of Brudenell's 18 holes.

Blind tee shots are not unusual here and observation towers beside several teeing grounds provide the opportunity not only to find out if the group ahead is safely away, but to survey the picturesque surroundings. On the fourth hole, after descending the tower, try to aim between the two white birches jutting out of the evergreens. A pulled tee shot ensures misery, because a line of trees intruding into the left fairway prevents a second shot in that area from being advanced with anything more than a short-iron. The 490-yard par-five rewards an accurate drive and strong second shot with a birdie. The broad Brudenell River runs behind this green, the famous red soil of P.E.I. marking its far shore.

Ascending the stairs of the observation tower

on Number 6, a short par-five, will provide the answer to why this hole is called "Twin Ponds." Like most of the on-course water hazards here, these ponds are brimming with black mineral water and any ball hit into them has no chance of being recovered.

"Needle Eye," the subsequent par-three, forces the player to hit a long-iron into a narrow-throated green braced by two huge traps. Like all the bunkers at Brudenell, these are filled with local sand, a coarse, red variety that can cause headaches for those unfamiliar with its characteristics.

Approaching the green on Number 9, assuming you have avoided the spacious fairway bunkers, notice the small island on which a memorial has been been built to the local pioneers. How many of them fell prey to the pirates that legend says once cruised up the Brudenell River is anyone's guess.

After completing the front nine, you are confronted with a wonderful par-three, one that has become Brudenell River's trademark.

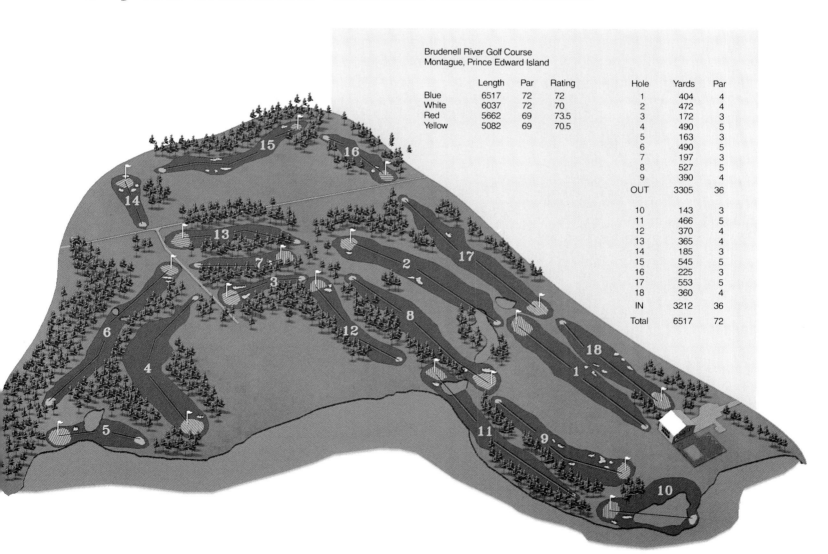

Brudenell River Golf Course
Montague, Prince Edward Island

	Length	Par	Rating		Hole	Yards	Par
Blue	6517	72	72		1	404	4
White	6037	72	70		2	472	4
Red	5662	69	73.5		3	172	3
Yellow	5082	69	70.5		4	490	5
					5	163	3
					6	490	5
					7	197	3
					8	527	5
					9	390	4
					OUT	3305	36
					10	143	3
					11	466	5
					12	370	4
					13	365	4
					14	185	3
					15	545	5
					16	225	3
					17	553	5
					18	360	4
					IN	3212	36
					Total	6517	72

Hole #16: 225 yards par 3

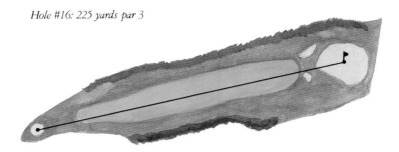

The Toughest Hole

Try to keep in mind the fact that major tournaments in the past, including the Canadian Tour's Atlantic Classic and the Canadian Mid-Amateur Championship, have hinged on the 225-yard, par-three 16th hole. Canadian Tour pros have consistently rated this the most difficult par on the course. Heavy rough, grassy mounds and traps mean a tough up-and-down for those who gamble with anything less than the right club. Aim for the centre of the green, especially if the pin is tucked in the far right behind a trap. Don't let the fact that the hole is nicknamed "Easy Pickings" mislead you.

Water comes into play on half of Brudenell River's 18 holes.

The 17th tee and its panoramic vista of scenic Prince Edward Island.

Constructed on a spit that extends into the river, this 143-yard hole over a pond plays into the wind. The most difficult pin placement is front-centre, and many players who try to be too delicate with their tee shot find themselves in the drop area shortly thereafter.

Like Number 10, the par-five 11th hole is short but dangerous. The sentinel tree in the left-centre of the fairway may draw your attention away from the river which forms the left boundary of the hole and the tall maples down the right edge. Only a long drive will offer the opportunity to safely go over the pond in front of the green in two shots. Like all the par-fives at Brudenell River, the result here can be a "4" on the card or a ridiculously big number.

A similar result is possible on the 12th, the hole that course manager Harry Simmons, a former scratch player, labels the toughest. The dogleg-right, par-four challenges from the start. The decision must be made whether to select a long-iron and aim for the white birch leaning out of the evergreens on the left of the dogleg, or to pull out a three-wood and try to carry the towering trees on the right. Option A means you will be hitting at least a five-iron

in from the brow of the hill — if you have stayed on the fairway and not rolled into the creek which meanders along the left side. Option B provides an eight-iron approach — if you've flown your tee shot the required 230 yards over the trees. The decision may rest on where your match stands at this point. In any case, the three-lobed green will not easily surrender to one putt.

The next hole presents another quandary, especially from the blue tee box. Playing this 365-yarder from way back in a tree-lined chute can confound even accomplished golfers. Hit a long iron at the birches which, as on several other holes, provide a reliable target marker. Or should you try to draw a three-wood around the corner of the slight dogleg? Perhaps your fate on the previous hole will help you make up your mind.

It has been said that Brudenell leads the unwary into a false sense of security and then rises up to seize them by the golfing jugular. Sound course management should allow you to avoid becoming another victim of this picture-postcard layout that should never be taken lightly.

Beaconsfield's well-manicured 18 holes have played host to many national and international championships since its founding in 1904.

BEACONSFIELD

Golf Club

Architect: Willie Park Jr.
Head Professional: Don Hachey
Manager: Keith McKeown
Superintendent: Mark Dufresne

One annoying aspect of living in Montreal 100 years ago was a bylaw that prohibited the playing of golf on Sunday. About the same time, it became fashionable for work-weary Montrealers to take the hour-long trip to the lakeshore near Pointe Claire, Quebec, so named because it was a "clear point" of land jutting out into Lake St. Louis. It didn't take long for the young bucks who had become enamoured of the game to discover they now could pursue it on the weekends. Arthur Tooke was one of a group who rented a few acres west of Pointe Claire in the village of Beaconsfield in order to satisfy their golfing urge in a most rudimentary fashion. While the young men were enthusiastic, they soon realized that they would need the financial clout of their fathers to make the dream of a proper golf course come to reality.

It fell to young Tooke to spearhead this initiative. "One day, we convinced my father to come out to hit a few balls," Tooke recalled many years later. "He had never held a golf club in his life prior to that time. Well, he hit the ball with his very first swing . . . enjoyed it . . . hit it again . . . and again . . . turned to us and said, 'Where can I buy some sticks like these?'" The elder Tooke, Benjamin, eventually became the first president of

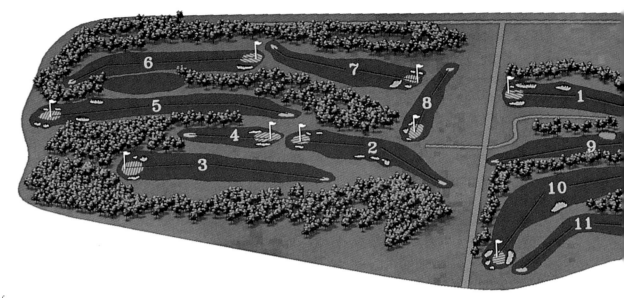

*Beaconsfield is a fine example of
a mature parkland course.*

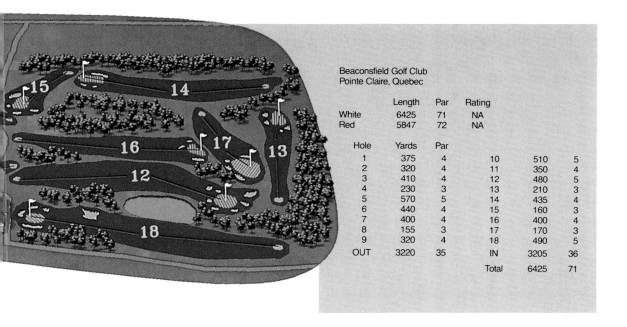

Beaconsfield Golf Club
Pointe Claire, Quebec

	Length	Par	Rating
White	6425	71	NA
Red	5847	72	NA

Hole	Yards	Par			
1	375	4	10	510	5
2	320	4	11	350	4
3	410	4	12	480	5
4	230	3	13	210	3
5	570	5	14	435	4
6	440	4	15	160	3
7	400	4	16	400	4
8	155	3	17	170	3
9	320	4	18	490	5
OUT	3220	35	IN	3205	36
			Total	6425	71

Beaconsfield Golf Club. Under his guidance, some 60 businessmen and golf enthusiasts formed the club in 1902, the same year they purchased the initial parcel of land for $6,500. The land they purchased, consisting of farmland and a quarry, was in an area that had been pioneered in 1640.

A quarry may not sound like the ideal site for a golf course; after all, rock is not usually conducive to the growing of grass. Huge limestone blocks had been wrestled from this quarry to build the massive piers for the Victoria Bridge which spanned the mighty St. Lawrence River. The site that surrendered these blocks now forms the base for the first, 11th and 12th tees and the practice green — after being painstakingly covered with a foot of topsoil. The battleship-sized outcropping of the quarry makes a stunning backdrop to the 15th hole, appropriately called "Gibraltar." Another fine byproduct of this mining was the construction of two stone buildings with metre-thick walls. One remains standing beside the 16th fairway and houses the offices of the course superintendent and miscellaneous storage.

By 1904, Beaconsfield Golf Club had been granted its letters patent, meaning it had official standing. To put its early years in context, the Wright brothers were experimenting with flight at Kitty Hawk, panning for gold was making millionaires in the Klondike and Henry Ford was sure the internal combustion engine would change the world. Alberta and Saskatchewan hadn't joined Confederation (Newfoundland wasn't even a consideration) and Edward VII was king. Six holes

were in play that first season despite the backward conditions; summer heat would open cracks in the unwatered fairways wide enough to swallow rolling golf balls. Expansion and improvement continued, however, and by 1913, Beaconsfield could boast of an elegant new clubhouse and played host to the Canadian PGA Championship, won by David Black of Ottawa. The nation's best female amateurs competed here in 1919, but fell to the incomparable abilities of Ada Mackenzie of the Mississaugua Golf and Country Club in Ontario.

Another fine player set foot on Beaconsfield the following year. Willie Park Jr. had won the British Open twice, but it was not as a competitor that he came to Pointe Claire. Instead, his mission was to improve the conditioning and revitalize the layout prior to the 1920 Canadian Amateur. He did such a fine job, bringing Beaconsfield up to a 6,034-yard, par-72 test, that he is listed as the course's architect of record. Park, a Scotsman, worked on more than 70 golf courses in North America, including no less than 10 in the Montreal region and is referred to as a "virtuoso golf architect" in the definitive book The Golf Course by Geoffrey Cornish and Ronald Whitten. Subsequent renovations have been handled by some of Canada's most outstanding designers: C.E. (Robbie) Robinson, Stanley Thompson and Howard Watson. Watson's son, John, is the course's design consultant.

Beaconsfield's tournament history gives credence to its enviable position as one of the finest competitive courses in Canada. C.B. Grier of the Royal Montreal Golf Club won the 1920

A former limestone quarry provides a striking back-drop for several holes at Beaconsfield, including the 15th.

The Canada Cup

On June 2-3, 1953, drawn by the aim of uniting a world ravaged by six years of war, seven international teams met at Beaconsfield Golf Club for the inaugural Canada Cup. The 36-hole team strokeplay tournament was the brainchild of Canadian industrialist John Jay Hopkins, a Beaconsfield member who founded the event, "for the furtherace of good fellowship and better understanding among the nations of the world through the medium of international golf competition." These ideals attracted a small, but high-quality, field including three of the four winners of "majors" the previous year: U.S. Open winner Julius Boros, U.S. PGA Champion Jim Turnesa and British Open winner Bobby Locke. However, the winners were a surprise package of Roberto de Vincenzo and Antonio Cerda of Argentina. With his two rounds of 70 for a 140 total, giving him a four-shot margin over Stan Leonard of Canada, Cerda also claimed low individual honors in the singles competition. But Agentina's 10-stroke triumph over second-place Canada (Leonard was paired with Beaconsfield head professional Bill Kerr) was less important than the good will established at the tournament and the resolve of all concerned to take golf to the four corners of the world. The Canada Cup was renamed the World Cup in 1967 and continues to be played annually around the world. Canada won the team title in 1968 (Al Balding and George Knudson), 1980 (Dan Halldorson and Jim Nelford) and 1985 (Dave Barr and Halldorson). Canadians who have registered the low individual score include Stan Leonard (1954, 1959), George Knudson (1966), Al Balding (1968) and Dave Barr (1983).

Amateur over Park's new track. Canadian Opens were held here in 1946, when George Fazio prevailed over Dick Metz in a playoff, and 10 years later when a flamboyant amateur, Doug Sanders, defeated veteran Dow Finsterwald, also in a playoff. As a historical footnote, that was the first Open to be televised. The Canada Cup international matches, now known as the World Cup, were born at Beaconsfield in 1953. The du Maurier Ltd. Classic, one of the Ladies' Professional Golf Association "majors," was held here in 1983 (won by Hollis Stacy), 1985 (Pat Bradley) and 1989 (Tammie Green).

But the competition that is closest to the roots of Beaconsfield is the Phoenix Invitational. In the pre-dawn hours of June 12, 1929, a defective electrical wire smouldered and then caught fire, causing a blaze that levelled the main clubhouse. Another scion of the Tooke clan, Fred, was club president at the time. "We will in future rise from our ashes . . . ," said Fred prophetically. Within hours of the fire, says the club's history, virtually every other golf club for miles around extended offers of assistance, accommodation and playing privileges. A member donated an impressive trophy, and in 1930 began the tournament named after the mythological bird which self-ignites, only to rise from its own ashes. It has been called an annual expression of gratitude to those clubs and courses which opened their doors and tees to Beaconsfield members during the period following the fire. The Phoenix trophy has been awarded annually since 1930 with the exception of the war years, 1941 to 1946. Players from all over Canada, the United States and Britain have played in the three-day qualifying and championship event.

Gently rolling with fairways defined by maples, the 16th hole typifies golf at Beaconsfield.

— Ile Bizard, Quebec —

ROYAL MONTREAL

Golf Club

Architect: Dick Wilson
Head Professional: Bruce Murray
Manager: Denzil Palmer
Superintendent: Ron Leishman

The early days of the history of golf in Canada are almost synonymous with the Royal Montreal Golf Club — the oldest golf club in North America, beating Royal Quebec onto the scene by a mere six months back in 1873. Royal Montreal's ground-breaking efforts didn't cease for decades. It was the first Canadian club to receive the "Royal" prefix (in 1884), the first in Canada to import an English golf professional (William Davis in 1881), the first on the continent to allow women members (1891), and it played host to the very first Canadian Open in 1904.

Now into its second century, the history of Royal Montreal is intertwined with that of the early settlement of this country. Golf had been played in the Montreal area by early fur traders, and a notice dating back 50 years prior to the founding of Royal Montreal invites members of the city's Scots community to a golf outing west of town. That the evolutionary process would continue to its inevitable outcome might not have been obvious in those days, although it is to those looking back.

The historic event came to pass on November 4, 1873, in the office of the Sidey Brothers, prominent Montreal businessmen. One of the founding members was Alexander Dennistoun, who served

as the first president and captain of Royal Montreal until 1890. The original site, called Fletcher's Field, was on the flank of Mount Royal and boasted six holes, which were probably sufficient for the 25 members. By 1895, the growth of both the city and the membership necessitated a move to the out-skirts of Montreal.

Longtime members fondly recall this so-called "Dixie" site on the bank of the St. Lawrence River in what now is the westend suburb of Dorval. By 1922, this course featured 36 holes — the famed North and South layouts — designed by Willie Park Jr., architect of other fine Canadian layouts such as Weston Golf and Country Club and Calgary Golf and Country Club. The second of two clubhouses built on this location, and completed the same year as Park's courses, was widely acknowledged as the finest in Canada.

In 1957, Royal Montreal moved for the final time to a 650-acre site on a beautiful island called Ile Bizard northwest of Montreal. The club engaged Florida architect Dick Wilson, whose work on West Palm Beach Country Club in Florida and NCR Country Club in Ohio made him one of the most sought-after course designers of that era, to build two 18-hole courses at the new site. Wilson was suitably impressed by the club's choice of property. "The great feature of this place," he said, "is the great sweep of the landscape. That vista of the Lake of Two Mountains is the perfect backdrop to these courses."

Head Professional Bruce Murray knows the courses as well as anyone and admires the Wilson design. "A general feature of the Royal Montreal courses," he has said, "a tendency of Dick Wilson, is that the bunkering of all the holes is more apparent on the front of the green and the entrances are very narrow. The key is that bunkers are positioned very close to the putting surface, which makes Royal Montreal basically a second-shot layout. You've got to hit the ball up onto the green, so the premium is on accuracy."

Royal Montreal is often thought of as pos-sessing only 18 holes — the renowned Blue course that played host to the Canadian Open in 1975 and 1980. Many golfers do not realize there are 27 other holes at Ile Bizard. "The Red course is just as good or better than the Blue," says Murray. "It may not be as spectacular because there is no water, but it is just as tight and testing. In many ways, it's similar to Scotland. The 13th and 14th holes, for example, have high mounds and well-bunkered greens. The fifth hole on the Red is an exceptional par-four — the Number 1 stroke hole. And Number 10 is a long, strong par-three with lots of sand and a narrow entrance to the green." As well, Murray points out that the so-called "Dixie" nine, which plays to 3,100 yards, is a collection of good holes that is often overlooked.

The Blue course is generally considered the tournament course. The group of the final four holes is acknowledged as one of the toughest

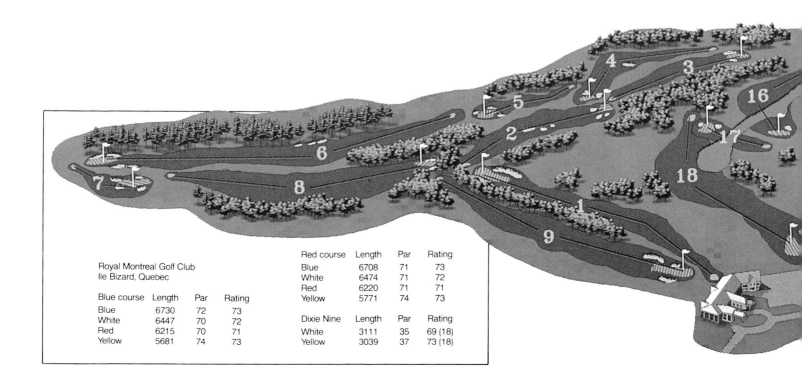

Royal Montreal Golf Club Ile Bizard, Quebec			

Red course	Length	Par	Rating
Blue	6708	71	73
White	6474	71	72
Red	6220	71	71
Yellow	5771	74	73

Blue course	Length	Par	Rating
Blue	6730	72	73
White	6447	70	72
Red	6215	70	71
Yellow	5681	74	73

Dixie Nine	Length	Par	Rating
White	3111	35	69 (18)
Yellow	3039	37	73 (18)

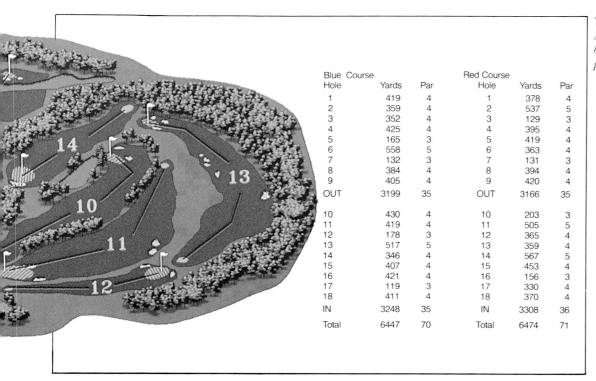

The 16th hole on Royal Montreal's Blue Course has been called one of the best par-fours in the country.

Blue Course			Red Course		
Hole	Yards	Par	Hole	Yards	Par
1	419	4	1	378	4
2	359	4	2	537	5
3	352	4	3	129	3
4	425	4	4	395	4
5	165	3	5	419	4
6	558	5	6	363	4
7	132	3	7	131	3
8	384	4	8	394	4
9	405	4	9	420	4
OUT	3199	35	OUT	3166	35
10	430	4	10	203	3
11	419	4	11	505	5
12	178	3	12	365	4
13	517	5	13	359	4
14	346	4	14	567	5
15	407	4	15	453	4
16	421	4	16	156	3
17	119	3	17	330	4
18	411	4	18	370	4
IN	3248	35	IN	3308	36
Total	6447	70	Total	6474	71

tests in Canada. Number 15, a 400-yard par-four with the wind generally following, may dictate a fairway wood off the tee, for a well-struck drive could end up in the lake. Hit a seven- or eight-iron over the water but make sure you take enough club to get to the green. The reason? Royal Montreal's greens feature narrow throats with heavy frontal bunkering. "You can hit to the middle or back of the greens here all day," says Murray, "and not get into trouble. Just don't be short, otherwise you'll have little puff shots over bunkers on every hole and those can wear you out in a hurry."

The 16th is "as good a par-four as there is in Canada," says Murray. The lake runs the length of the left side, so the better player will try to cut the ball in over the lake to the centre of the fairway. He still faces a four- or five-iron uphill and over a pond. Number 17 is a great par-three: caught between the water and a large bunker left is a small green that narrows severely at the entrance. Only a short-iron effort at 120 yards, this hole can wreak psychological and physical damage.

The finishing hole is a splendid par-four with an interesting tournament history. Jack Nicklaus, with a one-shot lead over Tom Weiskopf in the 1975 Open, splashed his one-iron effort into water at the corner of the dogleg. Although his heroic third shot (after taking a penalty) reached the green and he salvaged a bogey, Weiskopf made par to force the playoff which Nicklaus lost.

The Red Course at Royal Montreal: the par-three 10th hole requires length and accuracy.

The short 17th on the Blue Course severely punishes an errant tee shot.

Charlie Murray

History, of Course

Another Royal Montreal claim to fame is that only five head professionals, three of them with the surname Murray, have been employed here in 110 years.

Willie Davis was brought to the original site in 1881. (Recent research indicates it may have been Davis, not Willie Dunn, who designed historic Shinnecock Hills in the United States after he left Royal Montreal.) The others were Charlie Murray, a two-time Canadian Open champion, and his son Kenny.

The present head professional, Bruce Murray (no relation to Charley and Kenny), took over after Pat Fletcher, remembered as the last Canadian to win our national championship in 1954. But Jack Young holds the individual record: he served as an assistant professional here for more than 50 years!

Historic Royal Ottawa is a tricky
test, seldom offering a level lie
and punishing over-confidence.

Aylmer, Quebec

ROYAL OTTAWA

Golf Club

Architect: Tom Bendelow (Willie Park Jr.)
Head Professional: Tom Mann
Manager: Don Kearns
Superintendent: Steve Verrall

The roots of the Royal Ottawa Golf Club go back to 1891, in the last days of Queen Victoria's reign, just a few weeks before the death of this young country's first prime minister, Sir John A. Macdonald.

The first members were a handful of gentlemen — professional men, senior government officials and businessmen — who, a year or two before, had enthusiastically taken up the latest fashionable pastime: golf. They met at the elegant Russell House hotel, long since demolished, which stood in what now is Confederation Square in the heart of the nation's capital, and decided to organize themselves "for the promotion of this healthy and satisfying game."

Their first course was "a fine and suitable stretch of ground" covering 50 acres in the Sandy Hill area, which was loaned to them by Charles Magee, a real-estate developer and one of the founding members. The resulting nine holes, with their deep bunkers, ditches and a swamp, were laid out by William Davis of England. Davis is known as North America's first professional golfer, having been brought over to Canada in 1881 to serve at the continent's first golf club, now known as Royal Montreal. This original course played host to the first Canadian Amateur championship in 1895, won by Tom Hartley of Kingston, Ontario.

Unfortunately, the Sandy Hill district, a brisk walk from the Parliament Buildings and the city's business centre, was becoming more desireable and expensive as Ottawa's population grew near the end of the 19th Century, and the decision to move was made by the club.

Thanks to the enterprising spirit of George Perley (later knighted), a second-generation lumber baron, and his cronies, the club first rented and then bought 108 acres of farmland on the Chelsea Road just across the Ottawa River, a couple of kilometres north of Hull, Quebec. There were 12 holes at first so, by playing six of them twice, the members could enjoy a 5,200-yard, 18-hole challenge. At the fourth hole, the player was called upon to loft the ball over a barn. Since it now owned property, the club decided to become legally incorporated and obtained the necessary legislation under the laws of Quebec in 1901.

Shortly thereafter, the club's investment paid off. A cement company bought the property for $25,000, delivering the club a windfall of about $12,000. They used the money to buy the site of the present Royal Ottawa Golf Club on the Aylmer Road on the Quebec side of the Ottawa River. The club moved to this site in 1903 and, under the energetic leadership of Perley, now president, erected a luxurious clubhouse at a cost of $20,000. Almost a thousand guests attended the official opening in the spring of 1904, presided over by the

Accurate approaches are required at Royal Ottawa to take advantage of the quick, true greens.

Royal Ottawa Golf Club
Aylmer, Quebec

	Length	Par	Rating
Blue	6403	71	70
White	6171	71	70
Red	5865	75	74.5

Hole	Yards	Par
1	471	5
2	205	3
3	420	4
4	530	5
5	390	4
6	145	3
7	345	4
8	225	3
9	425	4
OUT	3156	35
10	330	4
11	157	3
12	150	3
13	445	4
14	460	5
15	435	4
16	390	4
17	340	4
18	540	5
IN	3247	36
Total	6403	71

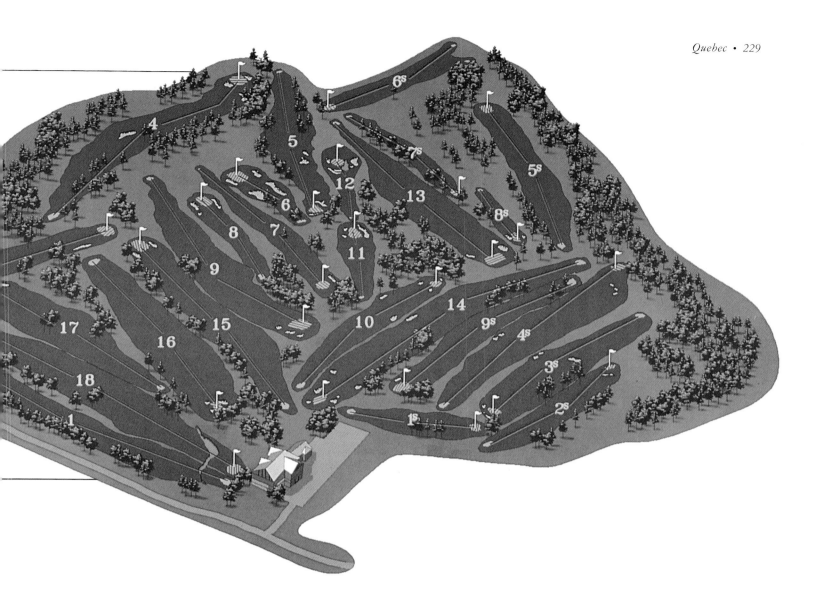

Governor General, the Earl of Minto. Five years later, the clubhouse was destroyed by fire. Its equally impressive replacement burned down in 1930.

In 1912, King George V approved the club's name of The Royal Ottawa Golf Club, a distinction conferred on only one other Canadian club at that time — Royal Montreal. Royal Quebec and Royal Colwood did not receive their royal charters until the 1930s.

Royal Ottawa's third course was designed by Tom Bendelow, one of the pioneer golf course architects in North America. It was later altered by, among others, Willie Park Jr., son of the winner of the first British Open. It is an old-fashioned course, in the Scottish style. What is lacks in length, it makes up for in topography. Its hills and dales, which virtually deny an even lie, and its relatively small greens offer an interesting challenge.

Bob Goalby, the 1968 Masters champion, was impressed when he played here in a Senior PGA Tour event in 1984. "It requires more accuracy, more clubface control and more skill than the big courses they're building today," said Goalby. "This is a thinking man's course." Local sports columnist Eddie McCabe once said: "It's a course which can crush a soul, reaching out unexpectedly to strike down the incautious swashbuckler who allows confidence to become overconfidence and carelessness."

One of the club's first professionals was John H. Oke, who won the first Canadian Open in 1904. The best-remembered and most-honored of Royal Ottawa's pros must be Karl Keffer, who arrived in 1911 and stayed for more than 40 years, winning both the 1909 and 1914 Canadian Opens. Tom Mann, who has been the head professional since 1971, comes from a golfing family. His father, Frank, was the pro at the old Tecumseh club in nearby Gatineau, Quebec, and his grandfather was the greenskeeper. Mann is one of two honorary vice-presidents of the PGA of America, the other being Lord Darby, president of the British PGA.

"This golf course is known as the toughest one to break par on in the region," says Mann. "It's very undulating and there are very few flat lies. It's got very fast greens, and they're not big. The rough is severe and if you get into it, hitting the green becomes very tough."

Royal Ottawa began as a gentleman's club, in the Victorian sense, although ladies have been active on the course and in the management of the club almost from the beginning. The gentlemanly tradition persists in an emphasis on good manners, appropriate dress and mutual consideration.

The club is often described as "prestigious" (Governors General and prime ministers routinely become members) and it is sometimes accused of stuffiness by people who judge it from afar, but newcomers quickly find it a friendly and accommodating place when older members recite tales of the club's legendary eccentrics who have given it life and color for a hundred years.

Subtle undulations can cause a quick three-putt on any Royal Ottawa green, including the 10th.

*Precise club selection is
demanded at Royal Ottawa's
11th hole.*

The Canadian Professional Golfers' Association

Robert H. Noble, a CPGA professional who served the organization in a number of roles for several decades, wrote the following on the occasion of the association's 75th anniversary: "On a warm, sunny 11th of July in 1911, a band of Canadian golf professionals, led by the legendary George Cumming, the head professional at the Toronto Golf Club, assisted by Karl Keffer, the head professional at the Royal Ottawa Golf Club, and 14 other head professionals and eight assistant professionals gathered at the Royal Ottawa Golf Club intent upon forming an association of golf professionals. . . . Cumming was the first captain and served until 1913; from all reports, he was the driving force behind the development of professional golf at the time. . . . It is the great Karl Keffer who holds the record for service as an officer of the association, for he served as honorary secretary-treasurer from 1914 until 1928. . . . Keffer became captain in 1934 and served until 1937, when he had the honor of becoming the first president when the Canadian PGA became an incorporated, non-profit professional association." Tom Mann, the incumbent professional at Royal Ottawa, continued this tradition of service when he was elected president of the CPGA in 1989. At present, the CPGA, the second-oldest PGA in the world after the British, has about 2,000 members.

*Meticulous attention to detail
makes Riverside one of the most
attractive courses in the country.*

———— *Saskatoon, Saskatchewan* ————

RIVERSIDE

Country Club

*Architect: William Kinnear
Head Professional: Larry Ewanyshyn
Executive-Director: Don Campbell
Superintendent: Doug Campbell*

If your image of the province of Saskatchewan is one of barren expanses of monotonous prairie trailing off endlessly to the horizon and beyond, then be prepared for a shock when you drive up to the entrance to the Riverside Country Club.

The name alone should give you a hint. Standing proudly on a plateau some 170 metres above the brawny Saskatchewan River, Riverside has the appearance of an oasis of calm — until you discover that its 400 male members and 150 ladies and their guests play more than 35,000 rounds in a six-month season. Those fortunate enough to set foot on its manicured fairways discover a world apart: Riverside's 18 well-designed holes wend their way through hilly, heavily treed terrain. So much for that stereotype of the Prairies . . .

Stephen Ross, executive-director of the Royal Canadian Golf Association, has visited dozens of courses coast to coast during his years with the RCGA. He calls Riverside "an exceptional golf course. Without a doubt, one of Western Canada's best courses and one of the country's best-kept secrets." Ross first visited Riverside in the late 1970s and has played it many times since. "It's one of my favorite courses anywhere. In addition to having a first-rate, well-conditioned course, it is fortunate to have a wonderful mem-

bership and top-notch management. It's almost impossible to find anything negative to say about Riverside."

The original course at Riverside Country Club was designed and built by a Scotsman named Bill Kinnear, who came to Saskatoon in 1909. Mickey Boyle's informative book, Ninety Years of Golf (An Illustrated History of Golf in Saskatchewan), notes that Kinnear was neither a professional nor a course architect. Apparently, his only qualifications were his Scottish burr and the fact that he had taken golf lessons at the Old Course at St. Andrews, Scotland. In any case, Kinnear laid out nine holes of the Saskatoon Golf Club in 1910, staying on as professional and grounds superintendent until 1946. He also designed and built the Riverside Country Club and served as the pro and superintendent there as well.

Though he didn't know it, Kinnear had started a bit of a tradition at the club. Don Campbell, the club's executive-director, has been with Riverside for an indeterminate number of years: "Let's just say I came here as a kid after the war." After dabbling at a number of jobs around the club, he wound up as its grounds superintendent. In 1969,

when times were a little tight around the club, he agreed to add the role of general manager to his portfolio. Then he took on the food and beverage responsibilities. No wonder the RCGA's Stephen Ross refers to Campbell as "Mr. Riverside!" He has divested himself of everything but the overall management of Riverside, passing on the mantle of superintendent to his son, Doug.

With that background, Don Campbell has an encyclopedic knowledge of the club and the intricacies of the course. Kinnear's layout has stood the test of time well, although Campbell credits two outstanding Canadian architects, C.E. (Robbie) Robinson and Bill Robinson (no relation) with bringing the course to the high standard it enjoys today. "Robbie came in here in the late 1950s with a master plan that made it much better," Campbell recalls. "And then, in the early '70s, Bill's plan added the finishing touches that took us to the top. We've planted many trees, as called for by Bill's plan. We've also added flowers all over the place — we put in more than 60,000 bedding plants every year — rock gardens, retaining walls, and so on. The course is manicured to the hilt, very picturesque."

Abundant water and trees on the fourth hole belie many Prairie stereotypes.

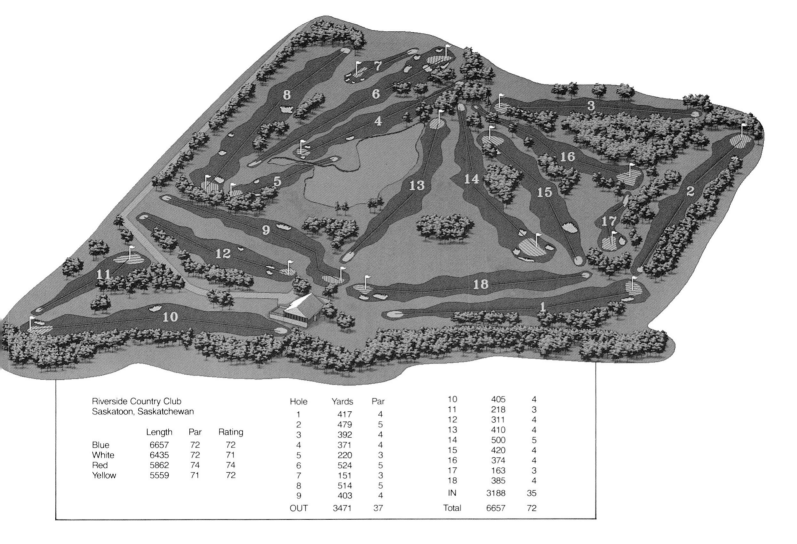

	Length	Par	Rating		Hole	Yards	Par				
Riverside Country Club					1	417	4		10	405	4
Saskatoon, Saskatchewan					2	479	5		11	218	3
					3	392	4		12	311	4
Blue	6657	72	72		4	371	4		13	410	4
White	6435	72	71		5	220	3		14	500	5
Red	5862	74	74		6	524	5		15	420	4
Yellow	5559	71	72		7	151	3		16	374	4
					8	514	5		17	163	3
					9	403	4		18	385	4
					OUT	3471	37		IN	3188	35
									Total	6657	72

Pulling the approach shot on No. 10 means the ball will come to rest in the river valley.

Another of Bill Robinson's suggestions was a seven-acre man-made lake that comes into play on the fourth, fifth and 13th holes. The lake represents the only water on the course, with the notable exception of the Saskatchewan River which makes an appearance on the first and 10th holes, causing "a lot of trouble," says Campbell. The river forms the righthand boundary of the very difficult opening hole. "The river and the bush on its bank guard the right side," he says, "and the fairway slopes left to right. The target area is about 240 yards out on the left, leaving a five- or a six-iron in. The green is big, with a bunker on the right and out-of-bounds behind."

The river is a factor on the first hole of the back nine, as well. "The 10th is another tough hole. There's a fairway bunker out about 250 yards on the right, and the river and bush on the left. Try to aim for right-centre for the best approach. It's anything from a five- to a seven-iron in from there. The green is very tricky and has a bunker, rough and trees on the right. There's another bunker on the left, and if you're left of that, you're down the slope in the riverbottom."

The secret to getting around Riverside with a respectable score is not in hitting the ball long, but straight. The layout plays to 6,800 yards from the tips and the smart player will try to keep the ball in the fairway at all costs, even if it means gearing down from the driver off the tee. What rough there is on this neatly groomed layout is treacherous and a ball in the trees will be found, but not advanced toward the hole.

As well, the prevailing wind comes into play on the fifth hole, part of what Campbell calls the most difficult stretch on the course. It may unnerve first-time players to discover that he considers the first six holes the most challenging of Riverside's 18. After surviving the first, the par-five second hole offers a slight reprieve — maybe even a birdie. But then, in rapid succession, come the 392-yard third hole, noted as an exacting driving hole; the par-four fourth with its distracting water threatening the tee shot; the muscular 220-yard par-three fifth; and the sixth, rated the Number 1 stroke hole.

In contrast to this crucial challenge, Ross recalls several holes fondly. His favorites include the dogleg ninth hole, with its blind second shot. "It's one of the greatest short par-fours anywhere. Your drive must be left, and there's

Hole #6: 524 yards par 5

The Toughest Hole at Riverside

The Number 1 stroke hole at Riverside Country Club in Saskatoon, Saskatchewan, is the 524-yard, par-five sixth hole. It is the longest hole on the course and, appropriately, is considered the best driving hole. To reach the green in two, you must bust your drive 270 yards and stay to the left. Your three-wood second shot must carry four traps on its way to the green. Most players will try to lay up in front of the traps, some 50 yards short of the green.

gorse left and right. Very links-style." Number 12 is another short par-four where Ross recommends a two-iron off the tee to ensure your drive avoids the punitive rough. "The 18th is a great finishing hole with a severe second shot. You've got to hit two very straight shots. You're hitting a five- or six-iron into a very

elevated, narrow green. There's a slope on the right that goes down about 20 feet, and if you're down there, well, forget it."

A short par-four, the 12th will punish those who use a driver from the tee.

PHOTOGRAPHIC CREDITS

CREDITS

Copy Editor: Leslie Gordon
Cover Design: Andrew Smith
Book Design/Art Direction: Nancy Roberts-Knox
Photography: Michael French
Golf Course Computer Art: Baynger-Northey Associates
Golf Watercolours: Paul Alette
Typesetting: True to Type Inc.
Colour Separations: Colour Technologies, Toronto
Paper: Provincial Paper (Baskerville Gloss)
Printing: D.W. Friesen, Altona, Manitoba